# Elements of Continuity

## Stone Cult in the Maltese Islands

### George Azzopardi

ARCHAEOPRESS PUBLISHING LTD
Gordon House
276 Banbury Road
Oxford OX2 7ED
www.archaeopress.com

ISBN 978 1 78491 695 4
ISBN 978 1 78491 696 1 (e-Pdf)

© Archaeopress and George Azzopardi 2017

*Cover: A pyramidal betyl found amid the ruins of the temple on the first terrace at the sanctuary site of Ras il-Wardija, in Gozo (see 6.0). (Photo: The Author).*

All rights reserved. No part of this book may be reproduced, in any form or by any means, electronic, mechanical, photocopying or otherwise, without the prior written permission of the copyright owners.

Printed in England by Holywell Press, Oxford
This book is available direct from Archaeopress or from our website www.archaeopress.com

# Contents

List of Figures .................................................................................................. v

Preface ............................................................................................................ ix

**1.0 Introduction** ............................................................................................ 1

1.1 Aims and methodology .......................................................................... 4

1.2 Defining and identifying sacred stones ................................................ 6

1.3 Earliest known literary and iconographic evidence ............................ 9

**2.0 Stone cult in prehistoric Malta and Gozo** ......................................... 15

2.1 Aniconic cults in relation to figurine-based cults in prehistoric Malta ............ 32

**3.0 Tripillar shrines or altars** ................................................................... 35

**4.0 Betyl amulets?** ...................................................................................... 41

**5.0 More betyls from Tas-Silġ** ................................................................... 43

**6.0 Stone worship at Ras il-Wardija, in Gozo** ........................................ 45

**7.0 A pair of 'twin' betyls** ......................................................................... 55

**8.0 A gilded betyl in the temple of Proserpina at Mtarfa** ..................... 63

**9.0 Conclusion** ............................................................................................ 69

Appendix I ..................................................................................................... 71

Appendix II .................................................................................................... 71

Appendix III ................................................................................................... 72

Appendix IV ................................................................................................... 72

**Bibliography** ............................................................................................... 73

Abbreviated titles .......................................................................................... 73

Ancient sources ............................................................................................. 73

Manuscripts ................................................................................................... 73

Digital sources ............................................................................................... 74

Published works ............................................................................................ 74

**General Index** ............................................................................................ 79

# List of Figures

Figure 1. Anthropomorphised stone betyl. From Sa Mandara (Samassi), Sardinia. Now, in the Museo Archeologico Nazionale of Cagliari, Sardinia. (Photo: The Author) ...................................................................................................................2

Figure 2. A male herm. Kept at the Museo Nazionale Romano Palazzo Massimo, Rome. (Photo: The Author).........................................................................................3

Figure 3. Stela with vase-shaped betyl in relief inside a niche. The stela comes from the tophet at Motya and is now on display at the Museo del Vicino Oriente, Sapienza University, Rome. (Photo: The Author) ....................................................5

Figure 4. Map of the Maltese islands. The map shows the main places mentioned in the text. (After www.geocities.ws/maltashells/NatHist.html). ......................................7

Figure 5. Table of Maltese chronology..........................................................................8

Figure 6. An Apulian red-figure amphora attributed to the Varrese Painter (mid-4th century BC). The amphora shows a betyl decorated with a ribbon and standing on a pedestal. The amphora is to be found at the Museo Archeologico of Agrigento, Sicily. (Photo: The Author) ................................................................11

Figure 7. A bronze coin showing the betyl of the Syrian sun god El-Gabal in the temple of Emesa. The betyl is shown inside a temple where it substitutes a cultic statue of the god. The coin is of the 3rd century AD. (Source: http://en.wikipedia.org/wiki/Royal_family_of_Emesa. Accessed: 1-3-2015)........................................12

Figure 8. Plan of the Xagħra Brochtroff Circle. (Source: Malone, Mason et al. 2009: 70 (Fig.5.11))..............................................................................................................16

Figure 9. The semi-anthropomorphised pillar-like stone from the Xagħra Brochtorff Circle in Gozo (left) and the one from Ta' Trapna ż-Żgħira at Żebbuġ in Malta (right). Both of them show the basic facial features while the second one was also stained with red ochre. (Left drawing: Steven Ashley; Source: Malone, Bonanno et al. 2009: 282 (Fig.10.46); Right drawing: Caroline Malone and Jason Gibbons; Source: Malone, Bonanno et al. 2009: 283 (Fig.10.47)) .........................17

Figure 10. Large spherical stone. It was found in the upper levels of the east cave at the Xagħra Brochtorff Circle in Gozo. (Photo: The Author).................................18

Figure 11. A stone pillar / betyl. It was found in the north-east corner inside the east cave at the Xagħra Brochtorff Circle in Gozo. (Photo: The Author) ............19

Figure 12. Twin-seated figures carved in stone. The one on the right holds a vase in her hands (shown inset). Found at the Xagħra Brochtorff Circle but, now, kept at the Ġgantija Temples Visitors' Centre in Xagħra, Gozo. (Photograph © Daniel Cilia).......20

Figure 13. Plan of Ħal Saflieni Hypogeum, middle level. (Source: Evans 1971: Plan 14B) ....21

Figure 14. A stone pillar from Ġgantija southern temple. It was found at the foot of a niche in the first right-hand apse on entering the said temple. Now, kept at the Ġgantija Temples Visitors' Centre in Xagħra, Gozo. (Photo: The Author)..........23

Figure 15. Plan of Ġgantija Temples in Xagħra, Gozo. It shows the locations of the stone pillar and of the conical stones. (Source: Evans 1971: Plan 38A) ...............24

Figure 16. Plan of Tarxien Temples at Tarxien, Malta. (Source: Evans 1971: Plan 30A)................25

Figure 17. Plan of Ħaġar Qim Temples, limits of Qrendi in Malta. (Source: Evans 1971: Plan 18A)................27

Figure 18. Plan of Mnajdra Temples near Ħaġar Qim Temples, limits of Qrendi in Malta. (Source: Evans 1971: Plan 20A)................28

Figure 19. Plan of Borġ in-Nadur Temple at Birżebbuġa in Malta. (Source: Evans 1971: Plan 1) ................29

Figure 20. A torpedo-like 'betyl' from Borġ in-Nadur Temple (left) and a similar example in relief on a stela from the Punic tophet at Tharros in Sardinia (right). While the present whereabouts of the former are unknown, the latter is in the Archaeology Museum of Cabras, also in Sardinia. (Left illustration source: Murray 1923: Plate VIII (19); Right photo: The Author) ................30

Figure 21. Plan of Tas-Silġ sanctuary in the area of Marsaxlokk, Malta. The plan shows the locations of the main betyls from both prehistoric and historic periods. (Source: Recchia 2007: 238 (Fig.6)) ................31

Figure 22. Table showing elements of aniconic cults in relation to the earliest phases of Maltese prehistoric temples. Elements of figurine-based cults are also drawn in for comparison, particularly in peak phases of the same prehistoric temples' lifetime ................33

Figure 23. Three upright stones at Borġ in-Nadur Temple at Birżebbuġa in Malta. Found in a semicircular niche, they may have comprised a tripillar shrine. (Source: Murray 1923: Plate XIX (2))................35

Figure 24. Tripillar altar in the temple of Zeus Meilichios at Selinunte, Sicily. (Photo: The Author)................37

Figure 25. Tripillar altar in the *sacello Triolo Nord* at Selinunte, Sicily. (Photo: The Author) .................................................................................................................37

Figure 26. Relief tripillars inside a niche on a stela. The stela comes from the Punic tophet at Tharros in Sardinia and is, now, kept at the Archaeology Museum of Cabras (also in Sardinia). (Photo: The Author)......................................................38

Figure 27. A possible pillar-amulet. The perforation at its end suggests hanging round one's neck. It was found on the surface of the forecourt in front of the Ġgantija northern temple in Xagħra, Gozo. Now, kept at the Gozo Archaeology Museum in the Citadel, Victoria. (Photo: The Author).........................................41

Figure 28. Miniature Djed pillars. The examples shown here were meant to be hung as amulets. They are on display at the archaeological museum of the tophet at Sant'Antioco, Sardinia. (Photo: The Author).......................................................42

Figure 29. The pyramidal 'cippus' / betyl discovered at Ras il-Wardija. Besides its pyramidal shape, the 'cippus' / betyl also stands on a base or pedestal. (Photo: The Author)................................................................................................................46

Figure 30. A pyramidal stone from the small sanctuary at Capo San Marco (left) and a pyramidal betyl from Tharros' southern necropolis, Sardinia (right). The latter is on permanent display at the Archaeology Museum of Cabras, also in Sardinia. (Left photo source: Pesce 2000: 220 (Fig.85); Right photo: The Author)................48

Figure 31. An artist's impression of the temple on the first terrace at Ras il-Wardija, in Gozo. It includes a cut-out view showing the interior where the pyramidal betyl might have received worship. (Drawing: Joseph Calleja) ...........................49

Figure 32. Small 'column' betyl with its surface rendered in the form of a spiral. It was found beyond and in front of the entrance to the cave on the fifth terrace at Ras il-Wardija, in Gozo. (Photo: The Author).......................................................51

Figure 33. An artist's impression of the 'column' betyl standing behind the two conical cavities on top of which it was found. The two conical cavities might have been an offering table from where, standing behind, the betyl could have received offerings. (Drawing: Joseph Calleja) .......................................................52

Figure 34. Figure with outstretched hands in a niche inside the cave at Ras il-Wardija, in Gozo. This cruciform and semi-anthropomorphic figure may have represented a transitional stage in the evolution from aniconism to iconism. (Source: *MISSIONE 1965*: Plate 83 (3)) ......................................................................53

Figure 35. A cruciform herm of the god Hermes. It is to be found at the Museo Nazionale Romano Palazzo Massimo, Rome. (Photo: The Author) ......................54

Figure 36. The two identical marble cippi each carrying a bilingual inscription in Punic and Greek. The inscriptions record an unspecified offering or dedication to Melqart / Heracles. The cippus on the left is still in Malta and is kept at the National Museum of Archaeology in Valletta while the one on the right is in the Louvre Museum in Paris, France. (Photograph © Daniel Cilia) ...................56

Figure 37. A marble cippus from the area of Santa Gilla in Cagliari, Sardinia. It carries a Punic inscription recording the dedication of the same cippus to Melqart of Tyre. The cippus is kept in the Museo Archeologico Nazionale of Cagliari. (Source: Amadasi Guzzo 2002: 178 (Tav.I))................................58

Figure 38. A betyl representation of Apollon Agyieus decorated with acanthus foliage on its lowermost part. As indicated by an inscription it carries, it comes from a funerary context. This Roman betyl dates to the Claudian period and is now kept in the Museo Civico of Padova, in Italy. (Source: LIMC II/2: 283 (Plate 27))...........62

Figure 39. The inscription *CIL*, X, 7494 recording repairs and renovation works to an old temple of Proserpina by Chrestion, the *procurator* of the Maltese islands. It was found in fragments on Mtarfa hill, in Malta, in 1613. (Photograph © Daniel Cilia) ...............63

Figure 40. Mtarfa hill (in Malta) outside the ancient urban centre and town of *Melite*. On the basis of inscription *CIL*, X, 7494 found there, the hill seems to have been the place where an old temple of Proserpina once stood. The photograph reproduced here shows British military barracks on the hill and was taken before 1918. (Photo: Author's collection)................................................64

Figure 41. A coin from Byblos showing a betyl in the middle of a sacred enclosure of an old shrine evidently dedicated to Hera. Dated to the early 3rd century AD, this coin gives testimony to the survival of aniconic cults in Roman imperial times. (Source: Moscati 1973: 76 (Fig.4)) ................................................67

# Preface

Stones can serve an infinite array of functions both when they are worked and when they are left in a 'raw' state. Depending on their function, stones can also be meaningful objects especially when they act as vehicles of ideas or instruments of representation. And it is, therefore, in their functional context, that the meaning of stones can be best grasped.

The stones dealt with in this study are non-figural (or aniconic) or, sometimes, semi-figural. They come from ritual contexts and, as such, act as a material representation of divine presence in their role as betyls. But it is not mainly the representational aspect of these stones that this study seeks to highlight. As material representations of divine presence that are also worshipped, these particular stones form part of a phenomenon that seems to know no geographical or temporal boundaries. They are of a universal character.

It is this universal character of theirs that seems to qualify these stones as elements forming part of the phenomenon of continuity: continuity across different cultures and in different places along several centuries. It is this phenomenon which this study seeks to highlight through a study of these stones. Hence, the main title of this study 'elements of continuity' with reference to these stones remaining in use as representations of divine presence and worshipped over several centuries and under different cultures.

As suggested by the sub-title of this same study, the Maltese islands are presented as a case study to demonstrate the phenomenon of continuity through a study of these stones. Worship of stones in representation of divine presence is found on the Maltese islands since prehistoric times. But the practice survived several centuries under different cultures represented by unknown communities during the islands' prehistory and the Phoenicians / Carthaginians and the Romans in early historic times.

# 1.0 Introduction

Like rock formations, individual stones frequently assumed cultic significance in human religious experience and in ritual behaviour. In the case of natural rock formations, this was often the result of their external appearance, sounds they produced, or their location in relation to places of religious significance which, often, they also came to share. But, as part of their ritual behaviour, humans could also make use of or fashion out individual stones intended for particular functions in the exercise of their rituals. The significance these stones assume needs, therefore, to be viewed within the ritual context in which they are created and utilised.

Such stones are known as betyls. They were often perceived – typically in Levantine and Aegean traditions – as the abode of the deity (or where the deity's power resides) or the deity's own aniconic representation (Budin 2014: 206-7; Crooks 2013: 5-6, 8; De Vincenzo 2013: 261, 265; Evans 1901: 112-3, 132-3). Symbols or inscriptions on or near betyls stating the latter's identification with named gods confirm this (see examples in Gaifman 2012: 212, 215-7, 220, 309; Wenning 2001: 80-4). Thus, betyls were considered as animated stones possessing divine or magical – sometimes, even demonic – power and were often believed to have fallen from the heavens, like the meteorites that were especially venerated as sacred stones in the Roman East (Gaifman 2012: 20, 24, 56, 74, 116-7, 308; Wenning 2001: 80). As a result, animated stones could also be iconographically anthropomorphised, generally with the addition of facial features, no matter how rudimentary they might be (Figure 1. See examples in Wenning 2001: 83-5, Fig.3. See also Gaifman 2012: 308-9). In this respect, such stones may be also considered as schematised 'statues'. As they shared the same nature of cult statues, betyls were, like these, kept inside temples (De Vincenzo 2013: 261). Such stones, therefore, not only enjoyed pride of place in cultic places but were themselves the object of worship: the so-called 'litholatry' (worship of stones).

When found in mortuary contexts, such stones could have served as memorial marks for the dead, perhaps equivalent to the Nabataean *nephesh* (Wenning 2001: 80. See also Budin 2014: 206-7). But, also on account of their association with the funerary sphere, they might have been even perceived

*Figure 1. Anthropomorphised stone betyl. From Sa Mandara (Samassi), Sardinia. Now, in the Museo Archeologico Nazionale of Cagliari, Sardinia. (Photo: The Author)*

as the abode of the spirits of the dead ancestors (or their aniconic representation), unless they represented deities protecting the buried deceased.

Such aniconic representations with their primitive and rudimentary appearance may sometimes be viewed as the antecedents, first of the semi-figural herms (Figure 2. Gaifman 2012: 36, 234-8, 305-6) and, then, of the artistically more developed figurative cult images (Gaifman 2012: 232-4, 305, 311-2). However, instances where aniconic representations are preceded by figurative ones cannot be excluded either (see Gaifman 2012: 310. Also 2.1 below). What seems to be certain, and as this study will confirm, is that aniconic representations remained in vogue for a long while alongside figurative or anthropomorphic representations of deities (see also Gaifman 2012: 310-1).

Less frequently, aniconism assumed other forms like a vacant seat or an empty space (Gaifman 2012: 32-3 (including Fig.1.1), 42-4 (including Figs1.5-8), 63-6, 71-3, 108-10 (including footnote 133), 164-9; see also 307-8). 'Empty space aniconism' was termed by

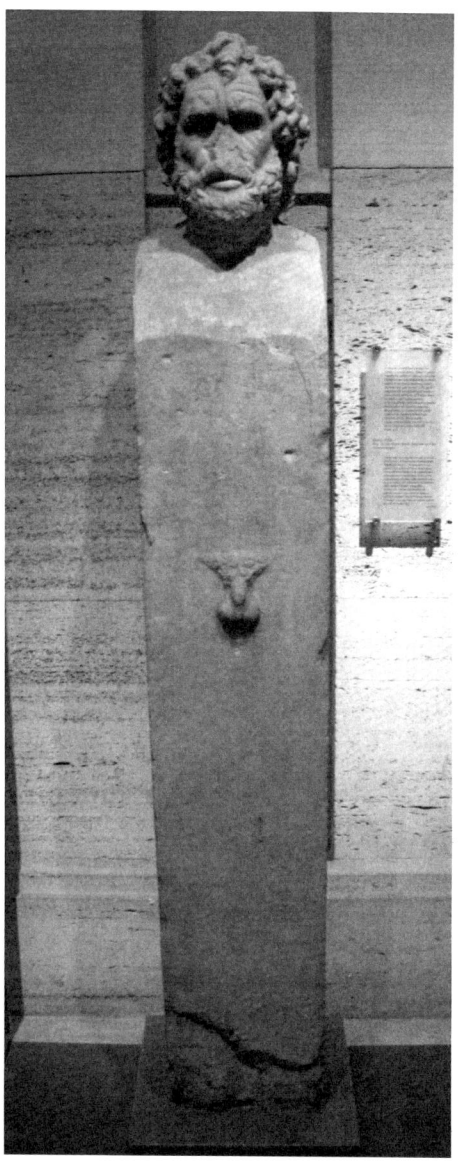

*Figure 2. A male herm. Kept at the Museo Nazionale Romano Palazzo Massimo, Rome. (Photo: The Author)*

Tryggve Mettinger, cited by Gaifman (2012: 29, 32-5, 165), to distinguish this form of aniconism from material aniconism discussed above. Alternatively, aniconism might also assume the form of a vase (Figure 3. Gaifman 2012: 125-8 (including footnote 201), 135, 306 (including footnote 13)) perhaps like the almost semi-figural (or semi-iconic) bottle-shaped betyl depicted in relief on two stelae from the tophet at Nora (today's Pula), in Sardinia (Moscati 2005: 209-10 (Fig.60), 212 (Fig.63)-3, 219; Pesce 2000: 196, 210-1 (Fig.77)). This bottle-shaped betyl seems to recall the ancient Egyptian semi-figural canopic jars. Both vacant seat / empty space and vase served as markers of divine presence (or presence of spirits of the deceased when in funerary contexts) but none precluded contemporary uses of figurative images like statues or figurines (see Gaifman 2012 citations immediately above).

But aniconism and figurative imagery were not always viewed as complementary. From a pagan perspective, aniconic forms were recognised as markers of limit (on account of their being non-figural) in contrast with the fully figural ones but, nonetheless, could co-exist with and complement figural forms or representations. Within the Christian interpretative framework, on the other hand, aniconic and figural representations did not complement each other but were rather in opposition to each other as the latter (i.e. figural representations) were viewed as agents of concealment (Gaifman 2012: 130). In fact, when criticising pagan imagery in his *Exhortation to the Greeks* (4. 52), the Christian apologist Clement of Alexandria (Titus Flavius Clemens) saw, in the veneration of stones, a purer stage when the materiality of the object was not hidden by artistic representation and thus, for him, the latter led to error (Gaifman 2012: 128-30; see also 308, 312).

## 1.1 Aims and methodology

Like aniconism, many other elements know no temporal or geographical boundaries. Demolishing temporal and geographical 'compartments' within which such elements have often been looked at, the emerging phenomenon is that of continuity. It is also in confirmation of this phenomenon of continuity that, to support the forthcoming arguments or to draw ethnographic analogies (see below), examples are drawn in from different periods and geographical regions.

*Figure 3. Stela with vase-shaped betyl in relief inside a niche. The stela comes from the tophet at Motya and is now on display at the Museo del Vicino Oriente, Sapienza University, Rome. (Photo: The Author)*

However, this reliance on different periods and geographical regions does not necessarily imply a process of diffusionism. It is understood that several phenomena – and the one under study is no exception – may develop independently in different geographical regions and in different periods often as a result of similar but independent social and psychological mechanisms that are at work.

Although this study deals with a particular type of stones with a specific cultic function, its aim is not mainly to highlight the nature of these stones, their meanings or their functions within a cultic context. Rather than that, it makes use of such stones, their meanings, and their functions in its bid to highlight the phenomenon of continuity which is connected with these cultic stones.

To address this phenomenon of continuity regarding these cultic stones over a span of several centuries representing different cultures, an island scenario has been chosen and, in representation of such an island scenario, the Maltese islands (Figure 4) are being presented as a case study.

Whilst aware that continuity of practice does not necessarily imply continuity of meaning or exclude changes in that practice, emphasis is being laid mainly on the phenomenon of continuity itself with regards to stone cult in both prehistoric and early historic times (Figure 5). One cannot fail to note instances where certain characteristic functions of these stones – like representation – appear to have remained largely unchanged. In such instances, therefore, ethnographic analogies are resorted to in order to glean meanings from documented examples of other times and cultures and apply them to those in similar contexts but which lack any documentation whether literary or iconographic.

## 1.2 Defining and identifying sacred stones

Often lacking any iconographic elements or accompanying inscriptions, certain stones may have, nonetheless, served ritual functions. They can be identified from the context – usually, a religious context – in which they are to be found, from the conspicuous location or position they usually enjoy, and / or from the treatment (like ornamentation) they sometimes

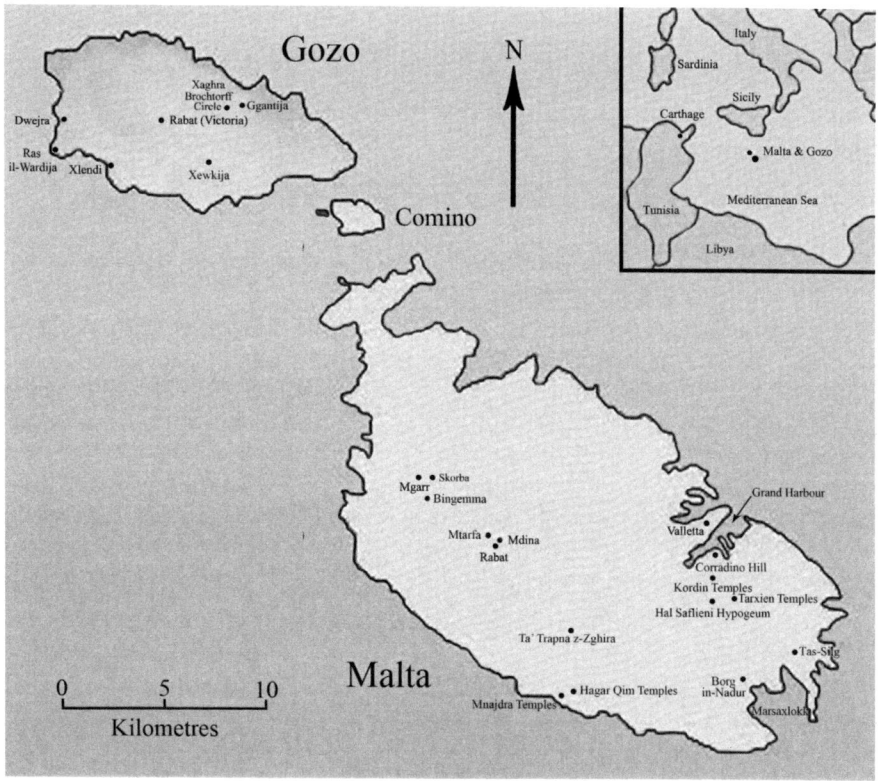

*Figure 4. Map of the Maltese islands. The map shows the main places mentioned in the text. (After www.geocities.ws/maltashells/NatHist.html)*

receive. These qualifying elements – namely, religious context, conspicuous location / position, and treatment – are shared by both dedicated betyls and dedicated statues, rendering them equivalent to each other.

Such stones are to be found in both prehistoric and early historic contexts. Their cultic significance or function can be more securely confirmed if, in addition to the above criteria, they carry also iconographic elements or accompanying inscriptions. But if these are lacking (particularly, in the case of prehistoric examples), those examples coming from similar contexts and which are supported by literary or iconographic evidence (especially examples from the early historic period) can provide ethnographic

| Period | Phase | Duration |
|---|---|---|
| Early Neolithic | Għar Dalam | c. 5000 – 4300 BC |
| " | Grey Skorba | c. 4500 – 4400 BC |
| " | Red Skorba | c. 4400 – 4100 BC |
| Late Neolithic / Temple | Żebbuġ | c. 4100 – 3700 BC |
| " | Mġarr | c. 3800 – 3600 BC |
| " | Ġgantija | c. 3600 – 3200 BC |
| " | Saflieni | c. 3300 – 3000 BC |
| " | Tarxien | c. 3150 – 2500 BC |
| Bronze Age | Tarxien Cemetery | c. 2500 – 1500 BC |
| " | Borġ in-Nadur | c. 1500 – 700 BC |
| " | Baħrija | c. 900 – 700 BC |
| Phoenician | | c. 700 – 550 BC |
| Punic | | c. 550 – 218 BC |
| Roman | Republican | c. 218 – 27 BC |
| " | Imperial | 27 BC – AD 535 |

*Figure 5. Table of Maltese chronology*

analogies that can make good for such *lacunae* (Crooks 2013: 6) as said above and as will be shown also below.

These stones may assume different sizes and shapes. Small ones might have been intended to be portable (see Wenning 2001: 81). Especially when worked, their shapes usually range from pillar-like to spherical, conical or ovoid but other shapes different than these are also sometimes encountered. In certain instances, however, and particularly (but not exclusively) in prehistoric contexts, they may retain their natural shape (Gaifman 2012: 11-2, 20-1) like the unwrought stone venerated by the Thespians and mentioned by the second-century AD Greek geographer and traveler Pausanias in his *Description of Greece* (9. 27. 1). Many are found fixed into the ground while others may be freestanding but they are almost unexceptionally always in conspicuous locations or positions. They may come from both urban and rural (or extra-urban) settings, could be also (though not quite frequently) decorated or carry some iconographic elements, and may occur singly or in pairs (Crooks 2013: 1, 8). Paired betyls are known, for instance, from Petra, in Jordan (Wenning 2001: 82-3).

## 1.3 Earliest known literary and iconographic evidence

As a phenomenon, aniconism is found in various religions (see, for instance, Das 2009), especially polytheistic ones or those which prohibit the use of anthropomorphic imagery of their god or gods, like Judaism (Wenning 2001: 79-80).

It is, in fact, in Judaism that we find the earliest literary reference for the use of such sacred aniconic stones. The Biblical Old Testament book of Genesis (28: 18-22) narrates an episode when Jacob, after having risen from his sleep, took the stone which had served him as a pillow, set it up as a pillar, and poured oil on top of it. He called that place 'Bethel' and vowed that the stone he set up as a pillar will be God's house and that he will make tithe offerings to God (see also Crooks 2013: 6; Evans 1901: 112, 132, 171). Labeled as 'God's house', the pillar may have been perceived as imbued or animated with God Himself and, thus, the place where the divinely-imbued / animated pillar was set up was called 'Bethel' which means the 'dwelling place of El / God'.

Related to the Semitic 'bethel' ('dwelling place of El / God'), the Greek word βαιτύλια seems to refer to open-air sanctuaries. In the 2nd century AD, Philo of Byblos identified sacred / animated stones as βαιτύλια, seemingly connecting them with the god Bethel. Bethel was one of the four sons of the god Ouranos who, according to Philo as quoted by Eusebius in his *Prepartion for the Gospel* (1. 10. 23), invented the βαιτύλια (Franklin (n.d.): 24; Wenning 2001: 80). The word βαιτύλια for (certain) sacred stones may also occur in the lost third-century BC work of Sotakos quoted by Pliny the Elder in his *The Natural History* (37, 135) (Wenning 2001: 80).

In an act of consecration / animation of a stone similar to the one described above in Genesis 28: 18-22, the Nabataeans poured blood of animals instead of oil on the sacred stone (Gaifman 2012: 117 (including footnotes 169-70)-8; Wenning 2001: 84-5 (note 13)). But in his *Description of Greece* (10. 24. 6), Pausanias notes that, at Delphi, a (sacred) stone believed to have been a substitute for Zeus and located at the central panhellenic shrine was anointed with olive oil every day and decorated with unworked wool at every feast (see also Gaifman 2012: 58).

Several depictions, particularly on seals and rings, show examples of betyls being leant upon or used like a cushion or pillow (Crooks 2013: 43-9. See also Gaifman 2012: 281) in the manner described in Genesis 28: 11, 18 (see above).

Mention is also made of pillars in a ritual context in another Biblical Old Testament book: Hosea 10: 1-2. Here, pillars are mentioned in literary parallelism with altars in the context of what looks to be a polytheistic religion. In this case, therefore, the several pillars might have represented different gods.

On several occasions, paintings on vases of the classical period also present standing stelai / pillars marking the presence of a divinity (Figure 6). These paintings are also themselves ancient witnesses to the nature of this phenomenon conveyed visually rather than textually. Free-standing pillars or stelai often make their appearance on red-figure Greek vases of the 5th and 4th centuries BC, sometimes even in association with funerary cult practices. But any associated cult practices or deities can hardly be identified if not with the aid of the background scene and inscriptions, if any (Gaifman 2012: 243-69; see also 310).

Columns and pillars associated with divinities make their appearance on coinage too. Most notable are the columns associated with Apollo. This coinage is mostly dated also to the 5th and 4th centuries BC although it extends to the 3rd and 2nd centuries BC as well. Occasionally, production of such coins with column / pillar imagery might survive even as late as the 3rd century AD, thus attesting to the particular significance that the column as a divine manifestation continued to enjoy in particular places (Gaifman 2012: 283-9, 309-10. See also below).

As indicated above, betyls continued to provide an alternative means of divine manifestation to statues well into Roman times. That the Greeks (at Pharae) still venerated stone betyls by the time of Pausanias' writing in the 2nd century AD is attested to by the author himself in his *Description of Greece* (7. 22. 4 cited in Gaifman 2012: 118 (including footnote 172)). In Cyprus, where betyls were typically associated with female deities (rather than male deities) since the Bronze Age, one encounters what is, perhaps, the best evidenced (both textually and iconographically)

*Figure 6. An Apulian red-figure amphora attributed to the Varrese Painter (mid-4th century BC). The amphora shows a betyl decorated with a ribbon and standing on a pedestal. The amphora is to be found at the Museo Archeologico of Agrigento, Sicily. (Photo: The Author)*

betyl at Paphos. This cone-shaped betyl, which represented Aphrodite, is not only shown on Roman coinage of that city (Budin 2014: 204 (Fig.10)-5; Gaifman 2012: 113-4, 170-5 (including Figs 4.20-3), 309) but is also mentioned and described in association with Aphrodite by the Roman historian Tacitus (*The Histories* 2. 3) quoted by Budin (2014: 205). Other examples include a third-century AD bronze coin showing the betyl of the Syrian sun god El-Gabal in the temple of Emesa (Figure 7. Gaifman 2012: 176; http://en.wikipedia.org/wiki/Royal_family_of_Emesa. Accessed: 1-3-2015) and an early third-century AD Byblian coin depicting a betyl in the middle of the sacred enclosure of an old shrine evidently dedicated to the goddess Hera (Moscati 1973: 76-7, Fig.4).

*Figure 7. A bronze coin showing the betyl of the Syrian sun god El-Gabal in the temple of Emesa. The betyl is shown inside a temple where it substitutes a cultic statue of the god. The coin is of the 3rd century AD. (Source: http://en.wikipedia.org/wiki/Royal_family_of_Emesa. Accessed: 1-3-2015)*

Stone worship also drew criticism from early Christian writers. In his work *The Error of the Pagan Religions* (20. 1) reproduced in English translation by Meyer (1999: 208) and probably written in the years immediately before AD 350 (Meyer 1999: 207), Firmicus Maternus admonishes the worship of the stone from which Mithras ('the god from a rock') was believed to have been born.

Already in the later centuries of Greek antiquity (when the Greeks were under Roman rule and came in contact with non-Greeks), betyls depicted on coins were generally shown within roofed shrines. These minted representations of betyls in temples continued to be particularly prevalent in the Roman provinces of the Near East, though found elsewhere too (Gaifman 2012: 169-78, 180). Thus, numismatic imagery of this period depicting betyls in the same way as figural statues within roofed structures / temples would have rendered the former analogous to the latter (Gaifman 2012: 174; see also 309). This would seem to confirm that these stones were regarded as objects of veneration analogous to figural statues (Gaifman 2012: 177).

# 2.0 Stone cult in prehistoric Malta and Gozo

On the Maltese islands, stones in the shape of a pillar or a cone and, sometimes, also in the shape of a ball (or sphere) that were evidently associated with cult are already found in prehistoric religious (and funerary) contexts. These stones can be identified as sacred stones (or betyls) on account of their evident association with altars, niches, or statues / statuettes, or on account of their special treatment, dimensions, or characteristics. On the other hand, those lacking these or whose associations are unclear and, therefore, their character is dubious, are being left out of discussion.

The earliest documented examples date back to the Żebbuġ phase (4,100-3,700 BC) of the Neolithic period in Malta; yet they come from funerary contexts where they might have been associated with ancestor cult, representing either the dead ancestors themselves or deities protecting the dead ancestors (see 1.0 above). The example found in the entrance (as if to highlight the sacrality of the burial chamber's doorway (see Azzopardi 2017: 42) or to protect the deceased buried inside) of the west chamber of a Żebbuġ phase double-chambered tomb at the Xagħra Brochtorff Circle, in Gozo (Figure 8), consists of a small semi-anthropomorphised pillar-like stone, otherwise plain but with crude engravings of the basic human facial features on its top part (Figure 9, left. Malone, Bonanno et al. 2009: 222, 282, Fig.10.46; Malone, Stoddart et al. 2009: 99-100). It may, perhaps, be considered as a primitive version of the Classical semi-figural herm (see 1.0 above). The other example (Figure 9, right), the surviving portion of which is restricted to the stylised top part similar to the previous', comes from Tomb 5 at Ta' Trapna ż-Żgħira, in Żebbuġ, Malta. Significantly, the whole surface of the second example – and, especially, the 'face' – was stained with red ochre (Evans 1971: 168, Fig.57, Plates 24 (3), 61 (7, 8)).

More extensively used throughout the Tarxien phase (3,150-2,500 BC), the underground burial complex of the Xagħra Brochtorff Circle yielded also an exceptionally large spherical stone measuring 75-80cm in diameter (Figure 10). It was found in the east cave's upper levels where it may have fallen from the surface of the site when the cave's roof collapsed (Malone, Bonanno et al. 2009: 266, Fig.10.37; Stoddart, Malone et al. 2009: Fig.8.82c).

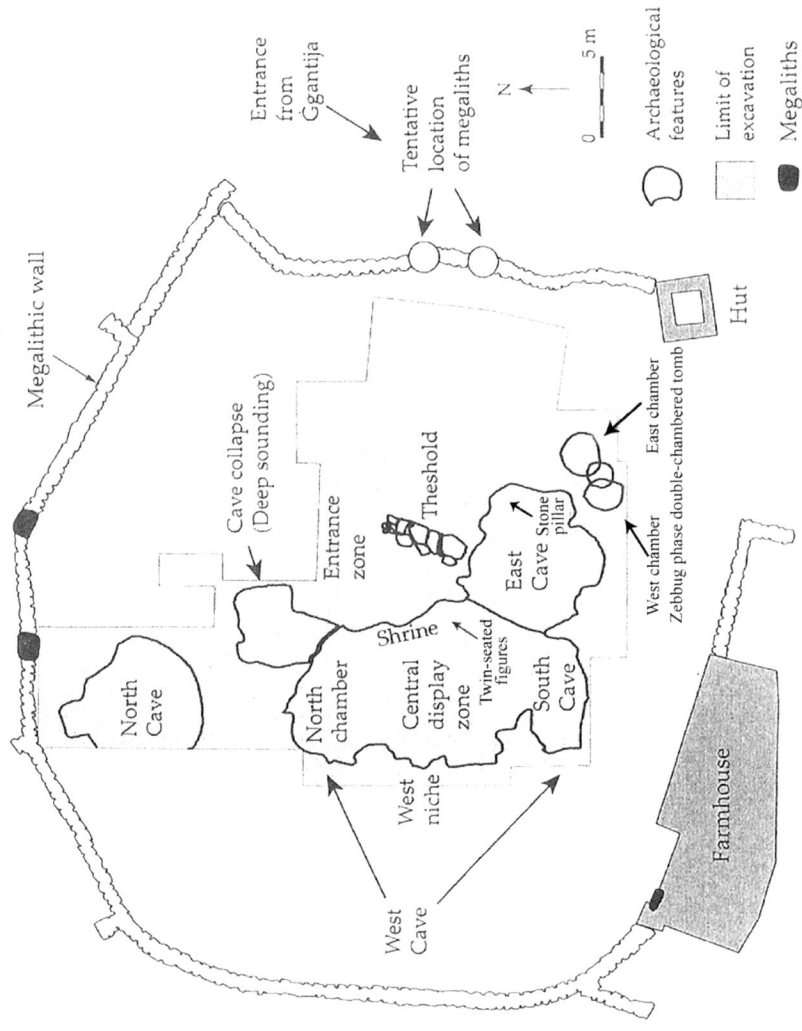

Figure 8. Plan of the Xagħra Brochtroff Circle. (Source: Malone, Mason et al. 2009: 70 (Fig.5.11))

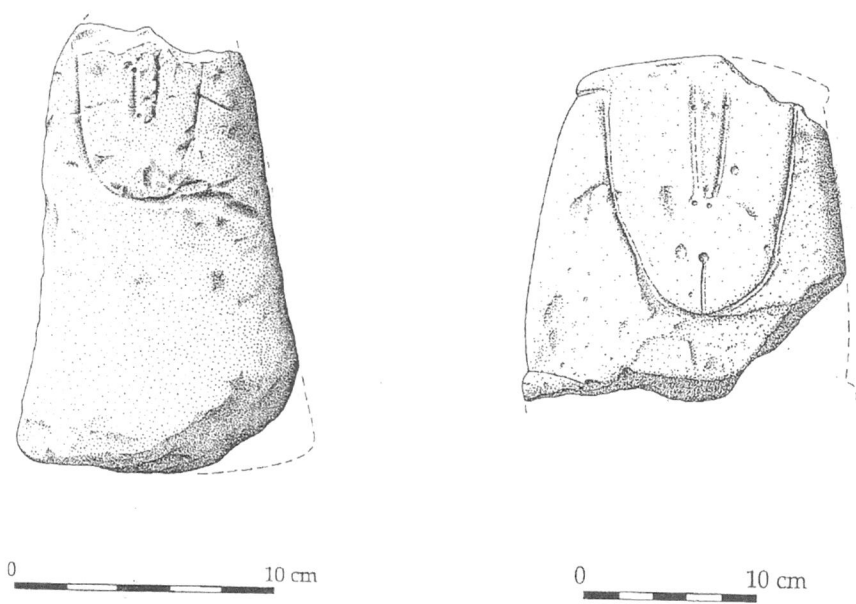

*Figure 9. The semi-anthropomorphised pillar-like stone from the Xagħra Brochtorff Circle in Gozo (left) and the one from Ta' Trapna ż-Żgħira at Żebbuġ in Malta (right). Both of them show the basic facial features while the second one was also stained with red ochre. (Left drawing: Steven Ashley; Source: Malone, Bonanno et al. 2009: 282 (Fig.10.46); Right drawing: Caroline Malone and Jason Gibbons; Source: Malone, Bonanno et al. 2009: 283 (Fig.10.47))*

From the north-east corner inside the same east cave came a stone pillar / betyl, at least 1.29m high (Figure 11. Stoddart, Malone et al. 2009: 194 (Fig.8.82b)-195, Figs8.66c-d). More pillar or column-shaped stones were also found in the burial caves and pits of the Xagħra Brochtorff Circle (Malone 2009: 426, 428, 431, 433; Malone, Bonanno et al. 2009: 283, Fig.10.34).

Perhaps likewise significant for the purposes of this study is a pair of stone-carved seated figures from the same underground burial complex. Probably dressed as two priestesses or priests, the two identical figures sit next to each other on a couch (Figure 12). Their probable priestly role (and likewise that of others represented by a number of Maltese prehistoric statues / statuettes showing a similar skirt design) can perhaps be deduced on the basis of the similarity of their skirts' design to that seen on the skirt of the

*Figure 10. Large spherical stone. It was found in the upper levels of the east cave at the Xagħra Brochtorff Circle in Gozo. (Photo: The Author)*

so-called 'sleeping lady' from Ħal Saflieni hypogeum (Evans 1971: 57, 62, Plate 36 (6-9)). In a ritual context, the latter might represent a priestess in a state of incubation or engaged in dreaming rituals to communicate with the gods or with the dead ancestors (Vella Gregory 2005: 49. Also as in Bremmer 2014: 116-7; Lincoln 2003: 3-5, 22, 37, 41, 44-9, 51, 54-6, 60, 68-75, 80-1, 87-90, 92, 121-2). Both of our identical figures lacked their heads upon discovery but one head was found close by and was re-attached during conservation. One of the figures carries a statuette (also with missing head but with different skirt design) in her hands while the other carries a vase (Figure 12, inset), likewise in her hands and in similar pose to that of the previous (Malone, Bonanno *et al.* 2009: 289-95, Figs10.54-6, 10.59). Shown in this 'parallel' and complementary manner, the statuette and vase might have been interchangeable (and contemporary) representations of a deity or of the spirit of a dead ancestor. If so, this may suggest that the vase may have been itself an aniconic representation or marker of either a divinity

*Figure 11. A stone pillar / betyl. It was found in the north-east corner inside the east cave at the Xagħra Brochtorff Circle in Gozo. (Photo: The Author)*

or, being in a funerary context, of the spirit of a dead ancestor while the statuette would have been its contemporary figurative version (see 1.0 above). On the other hand, the identical mutilation of all three heads is highly unlikely to have been accidental. It might have been, therefore, a deliberate act, perhaps to annihilate the figures' respective identities. It could have also been part of a desacralisation exercise (perhaps, involving also deposition, maintaining them within the sacred precinct on account of their sacred character) and / or to prevent their re-use upon termination of the associated cult or closure / change of use of the site. Such deliberate mutilations often took place in ritual contexts for similar reasons (Glinister 2000: 56-60, 67-70).

*Figure 12. Twin-seated figures carved in stone. The one on the right holds a vase in her hands (shown inset). Found at the Xagħra Brochtorff Circle but, now, kept at the Ġgantija Temples Visitors' Centre in Xagħra, Gozo. (Photograph © Daniel Cilia)*

Likewise used mainly during the Tarxien phase, the other prehistoric funerary hypogeum of Ħal Saflieni, in Malta (Figure 13), also yielded a stone pillar and a relatively large but slightly flattened stone sphere in room 12 (Evans 1971: 48) and seven more stone spheres and four stone pillars – all of varying sizes – in hall 24 (Evans 1971: 53). In an entirely rock-cut environment like that of the Ħal Saflieni underground burial complex, none of the mentioned stone spheres could have been used as rollers to transport huge stone blocks as claimed, for example, in respect of those sometimes found on ground-surface built temple sites (see below).

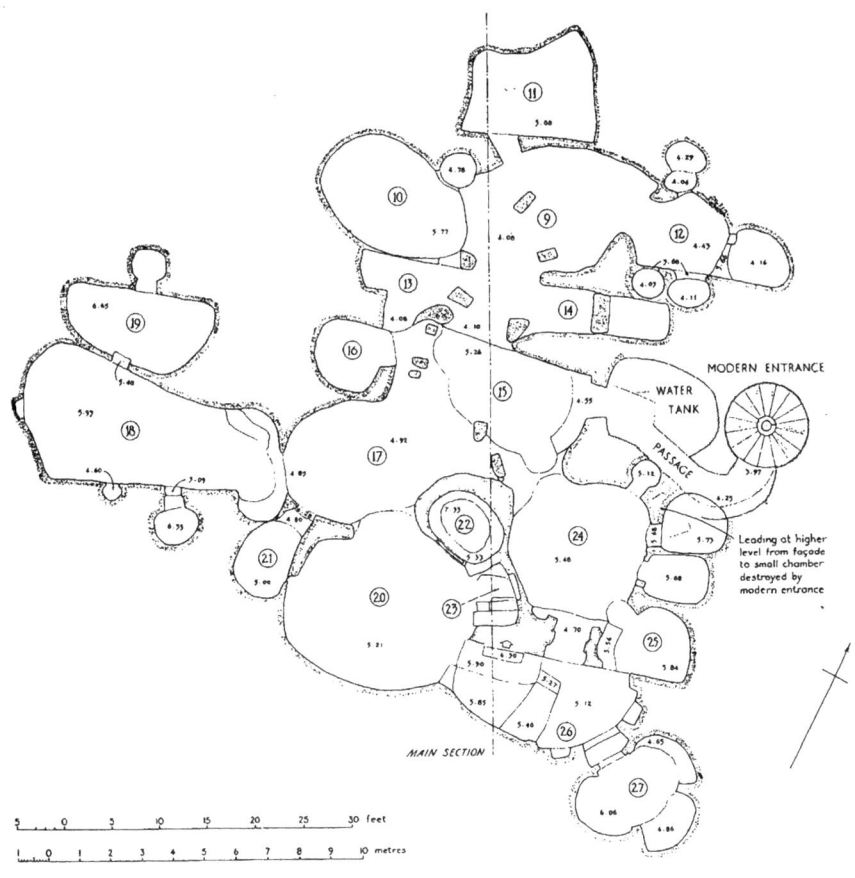

Figure 13. Plan of Ħal Saflieni Hypogeum, middle level. (Source: Evans 1971: Plan 14B)

More examples come from the temples. A c.1m-high stone pillar (Figure 14) was found at the foot of a niche along with two limestone heads in the first right-hand apse on entering the Ġgantija southern temple. This temple is one of two adjacent temples built in their present form during the Ġgantija phase (3,600-3,200 BC) at Ġgantija in Xagħra, Gozo (Figure 15. Evans 1971: 174-5, 179-80, 184, Plates 25 (5), 28 (4), 62 (1-7)). In addition to the above-mentioned pillar, at least four conical stones could be identified at the Ġgantija temples on the basis of pictorial evidence provided by a number of coloured drawings executed by Charles de Brochtorff during the 1820s (NLM, MS 1161: Plates 5, 8-10, 13-17). Whilst acknowledging any likely displacement taking place along the course of time, one conical stone could be seen in front of what looks to have been an altar in the rear apse of the adjacent northern temple (Plates 13-15) and a second one is shown in the first left-hand apse on entering the same temple (Plates 16-17). Two more are located in the larger southern temple: one is seen in the first left-hand apse, next to the second threshold containing 'libation' holes, on entering the temple (Plates 9-10) while another one is shown in the passageway on approaching the rearmost apse that may have provided the setting for another altar (Plates 5, 8). Although the last conical stone's association with ritual is less clear, its shape's close resemblance to that of the previous ones renders it likely to have similarly been of a betylic nature.

A single spherical stone comparable in size to the one found at the Xagħra Brochtorff Circle (see above) was to be seen amongst the remains of a prehistoric temple in Xewkija, Gozo. These remains were later destroyed by the building thereat of the parish church (Abela 1647: 119; Evans 1971: 191).

The Tarxien temple complex in Malta (Figure 16) yielded two cylindrical stones: one was found standing in front of a so-called 'divining block' near the eastern end of the temple's facade (Evans 1971: 118, Plate 14 (6)) while the other was found in the north-west corner of apse 3, about 50cm from altar γ. The latter's surface was decorated with drilled holes (Evans 1971: 122). A 17cm-high 'obelisk-like stone' with pitted decoration came from court 1 where it was found behind a statue (Evans 1971: 145, Plate 51 (4)) as if being replaced by this statue but, at the same time, was maintained on account of its sacred character (as in Glinister 2000: 56-60, 67-70). A stone cone with a sherd beneath it was also found behind the right foot of the same statue (Evans 1971: 151-2), perhaps bearing the same significance as the 'obelisk-like stone'. Another stone cone was found with a flattened back as if to be allowed to stand against a wall while its whole front was painted with red pigment (Evans 1971: 145, Plate 51 (5)).

Three more stone pillars come from Ħaġar Qim temple complex (Figure 17). Fragments of a stone pillar associated with fragments of a stone basin were found in apse 3 (Evans 1971: 83). A 2m-high pillar was set in niche 15, on the exterior. Immediately in front of this pillar, stood what looks like a kind of altar consisting of a carefully smoothed, upright slab broadening towards the top and having drilled decoration on its front (Evans 1971: 84, Plate 9 (1)). Another pillar stood within the right apse of room 10 (Evans 1971: 85). A roughly rounded massive stone sphere was reported to have been also found amid the ruins in subsidiary building 2 (Evans 1971: 87) which is very likely to have been another cult structure perhaps preceding the main temple complex (Evans

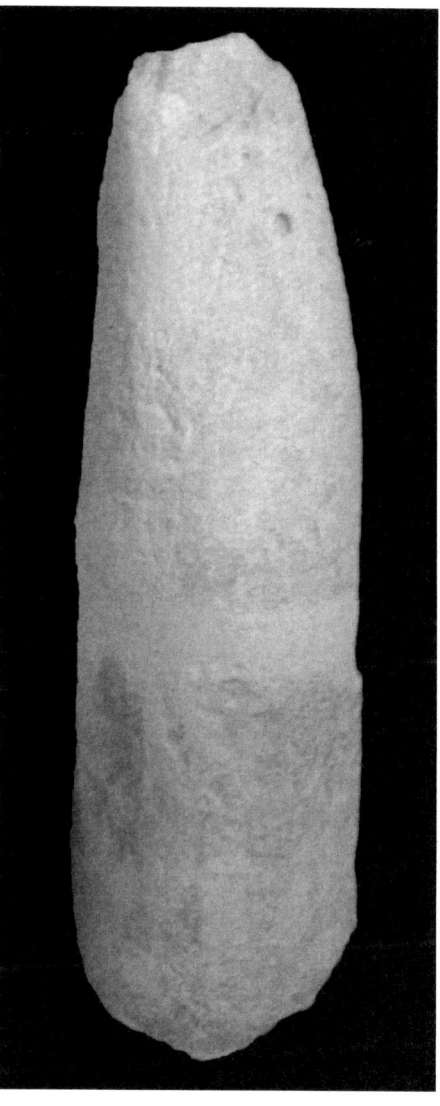

Figure 14. A stone pillar from Ġgantija southern temple. It was found at the foot of a niche in the first right-hand apse on entering the said temple. Now, kept at the Ġgantija Temples Visitors' Centre in Xagħra, Gozo. (Photo: The Author)

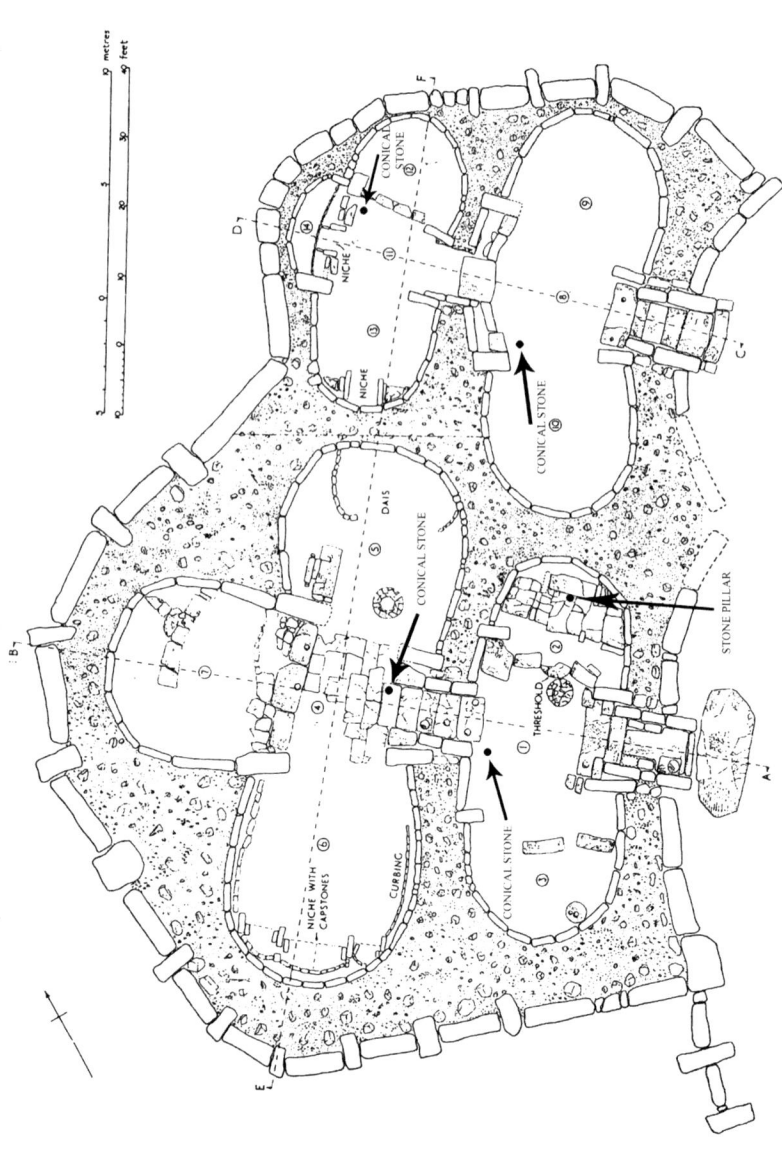

Figure 15. Plan of Ġgantija Temples in Xagħra, Gozo. It shows the locations of the stone pillar and of the conical stones. (Source: Evans 1971: Plan 38A)

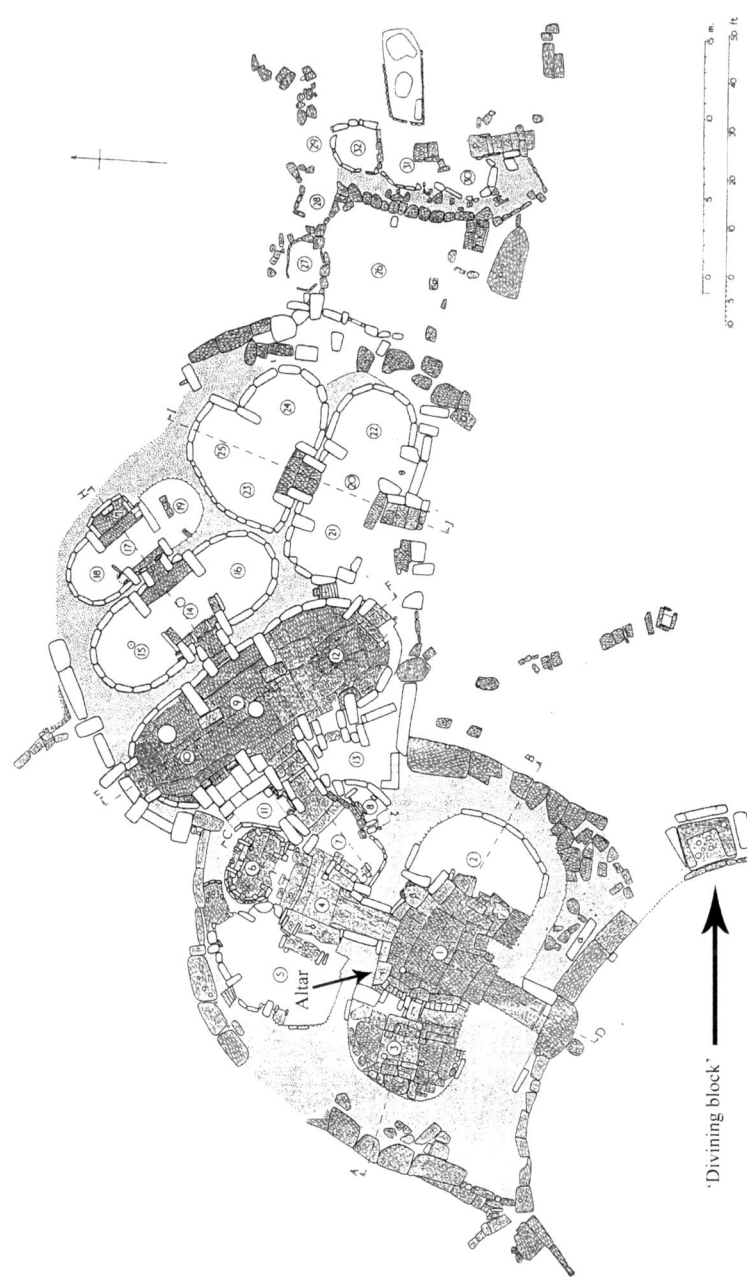

Figure 16. Plan of Tarxien Temples at Tarxien, Malta. (Source: Evans 1971: Plan 30A)

1971: 90). Nineteen more small stone spheres (ranging in diameter from 2.8cm to 7.5cm) are also reported from the main complex (Evans 1971: 94).

Another very large stone sphere (diameter: *c.* 80cm) and a conical stone were found in nearby Mnajdra temples (Figure 18). The former was found 'in a small recess' (perhaps, a niche) near the eastern orthostat forming part of the doorway leading into intramural room 6 (Evans 1971: 99). The latter came from the so-called 'pillar niche' in room 5. It was unearthed from around the pillar supporting the said niche (Evans 1971: 97).

The temple complex of Kordin is perhaps best known to have yielded exclusively cultic stones of all three types (i.e. pillar-like, conical, and spherical) in contrast to a complete absence of statuettes. Small stone pillars and a small conical stone (5.7cm high and 3cm in diameter at its base) with two small round depressions lying side by side near its apex are reported from Kordin II (East). Having been described as a possible rough statuette (Evans 1971: 78), the latter might have been a semi-anthropomorphised conical stone. Kordin III (South) yielded what was described as a 'betyl-like stone' found in the filling of room 3 (Evans 1971: 74) while a number of spherical stones (averaging 5cm in diameter) were also recorded from the same south temple (Evans 1971: 80).

More stones described as 'betyls' are reported from Borġ in-Nadur temple (Figure 19). One was found with part of a stone bowl in the filling of the western wall of the temple's 'oval' area (Evans 1971: 9) while four others were found respectively in loose earth near area 7 (Evans 1971: 10), in a corner to the east in apse 11 where, in a niche's filling, a small pillar (possibly, the 'betyl' illustrated in Murray (1923: Plate VIII (20))) was also found (Evans 1971: 11), in the north-west apse 14 (Evans 1971: 12), and in chamber 16, along with a stone bowl fragment and animal bones (Evans 1971: 13) where, together with these, it (i.e. the 'betyl') may have, thus, constituted a structured deposition. The latter is a torpedo-like 'betyl' (Figure 20, left) and is illustrated in Murray (1923: Plate VIII (19)). It looks very similar to an example appearing in relief inside a niche on a stela from the Punic tophet at Tharros in Sardinia (Figure 20, right) and, now, in the Archaeology Museum of Cabras (also in Sardinia), possibly suggesting a common source of inspiration or continuity of a religious tradition. Our

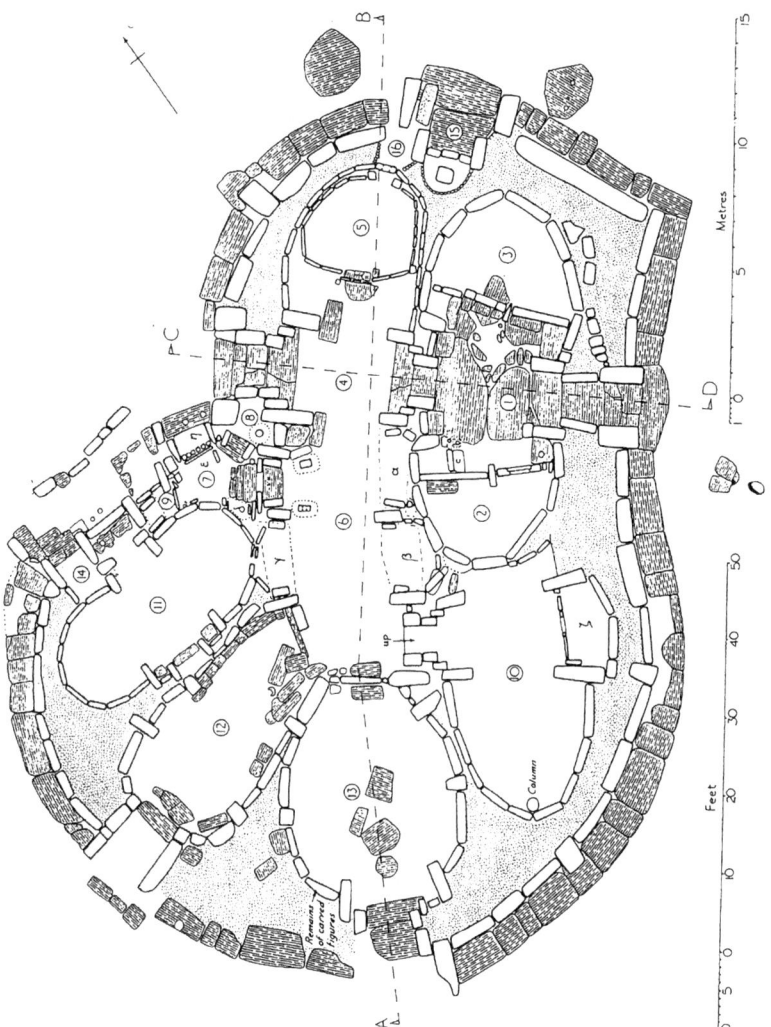

Figure 17. Plan of Ħaġar Qim Temples, limits of Qrendi in Malta. (Source: Evans 1971: Plan 18A)

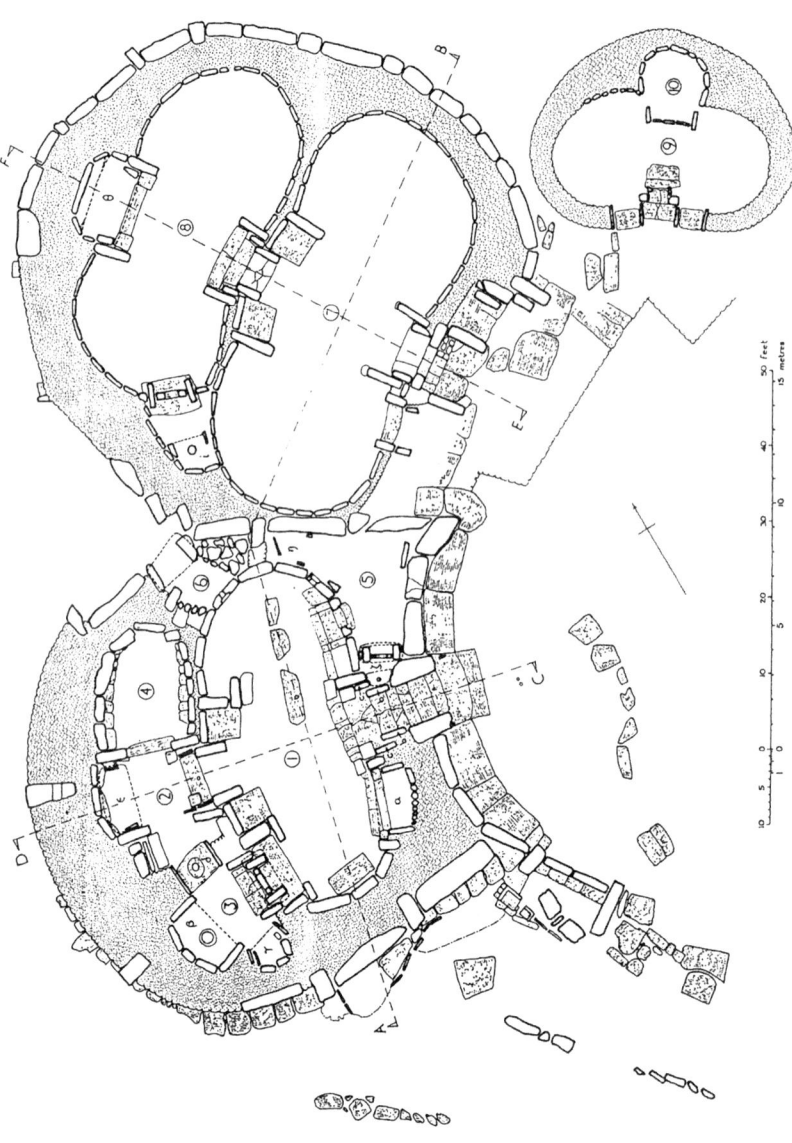

Figure 18. Plan of Mnajdra Temples near Ħaġar Qim Temples, limits of Qrendi in Malta. (Source: Evans 1971: Plan 20A)

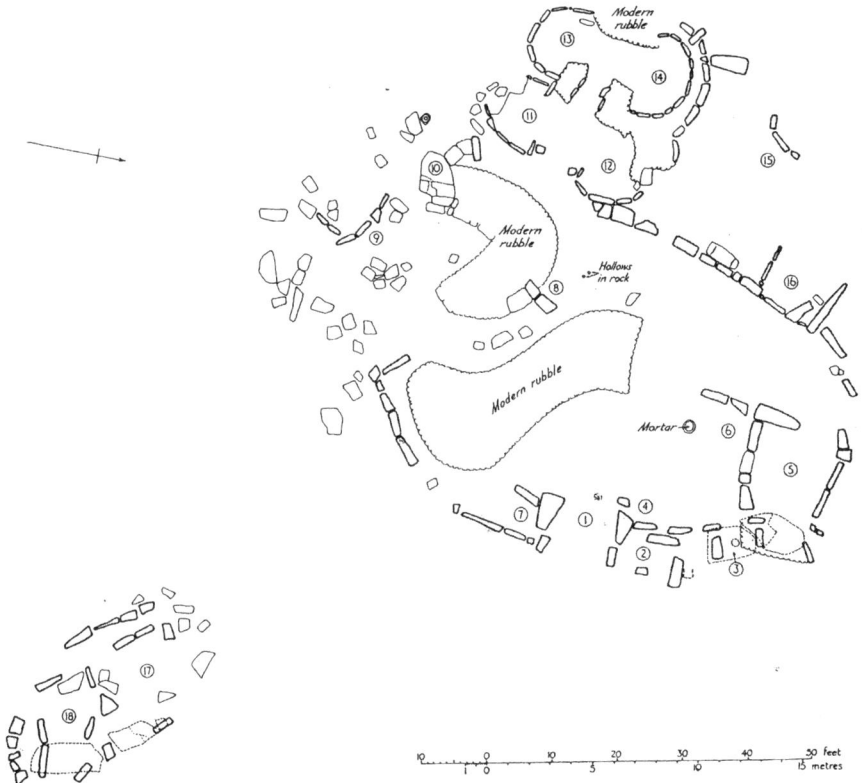

*Figure 19. Plan of Borġ in-Nadur Temple at Birżebbuġa in Malta. (Source: Evans 1971: Plan 1)*

last four examples (including the small pillar) were also variably associated with Bronze Age pottery.

Two more betyls come from Tas-Silġ sanctuary in the area of Marsaxlokk (Figure 21). They come respectively from Areas 3 and 6 of the sanctuary complex. The betyl found in Area 3 was fixed in a dug hole and there was red earth on its eastern side. The visible height of this betyl was 1.65m but it was split in three matching pieces that were still clustered together *in situ* as at the moment of breakage (*Missione 1970*: 55). It cannot be excluded that this breakage might have been deliberate, perhaps following the introduction of new cults or changes in religious ideology. Another

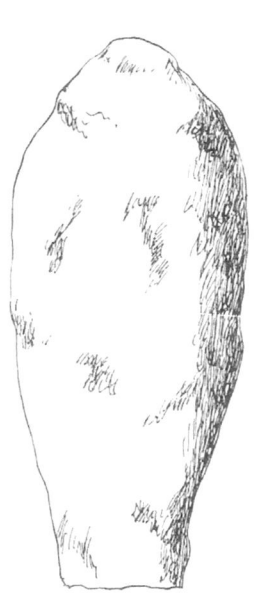 

*Figure 20. A torpedo-like 'betyl' from Borġ in-Nadur Temple (left) and a similar example in relief on a stela from the Punic tophet at Tharros in Sardinia (right). While the present whereabouts of the former are unknown, the latter is in the Archaeology Museum of Cabras, also in Sardinia. (Left illustration source: Murray 1923: Plate VIII (19); Right photo: The Author)*

similar betyl (about 1.30m high) was found in Area 6. It stood next to and on the western side of a stone basin that might have been used for ritual cleansing. This betyl was also split in two matching pieces as a result of *in situ* and, perhaps, deliberate breakage; possibly also for similar reasons as above (*Missione 1968*: 39-40, 78, 118-9, Plate 2 (2-3)). Fragments of cylindrical betyls (described by the excavators as 'votive' and, therefore, presumably small) were also found in the area (*Missione 1968*: 119). Fragmentation of these cylindrical betyls might have been likewise deliberate for similar reasons. The earliest known occupation of the Tas-Silġ site goes back to

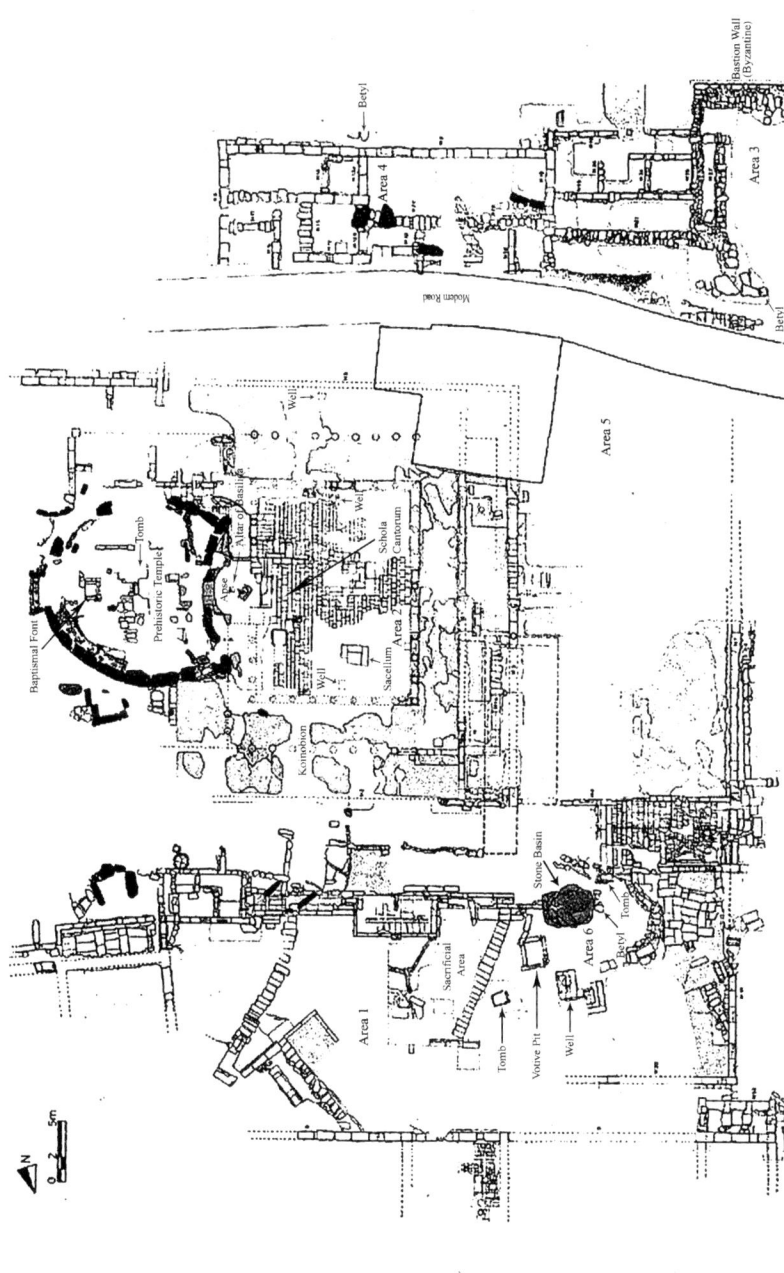

Figure 21. Plan of Tas-Silġ sanctuary in the area of Marsaxlokk, Malta. The plan shows the locations of the main betyls from both prehistoric and historic periods. (Source: Recchia 2007: 238 (Fig.6))

the prehistoric Tarxien phase when a megalithic temple was built there but ritual activity extended beyond the temple too. Later, this prehistoric temple was modified and additional structures (both inside and beyond the temple) were built to accommodate new rituals in both later prehistoric and historic periods (*Missione 1963-70*). For instance, the zone containing the basin and the betyl next to it (in Area 6) remained in use until the 3rd or 2nd century BC (*Missione 1968*: 44-5).

## 2.1 Aniconic cults in relation to figurine-based cults in prehistoric Malta

The picture attained so far seems to suggest a scenario whereby, in contrast to the earlier Red Skorba phase (4,400-4,100 BC) when cultic worship employed the earliest known cultic figurines known on the Maltese islands (Evans 1971: 37-8, Plate 34 (2)), different representational tastes or choices perhaps attributed to a particular group (or a new wave or waves?) of people in the beginning of the Temple Period (Żebbuġ and Ġgantija phases) may have introduced aniconic cults (characteristic of the Eastern Mediterranean and the Aegean area (Budin 2014: 206-7; De Vincenzo 2013: 265. See also Gaifman 2012: 305) though not necessarily diffused from there

| Site | Earliest Phase | Peak Phase | Pillars / columns | Cones | Spheres | Anthr. figurines (including fragments) | Reference |
|---|---|---|---|---|---|---|---|
| Skorba | Għar Dalam | (Red) Skorba | / | / | / | 9 | Evans 1971: 37-8, Plate 34 (2) |
| Xagħra Brochtorff Circle | Żebbuġ | Tarxien | 7 | / | 1 | 64 (excluding the rather aniconic ones from Tarxien Cemetery contexts) | Malone, Stoddart et al. (eds.) 2009: 100, 166, 194-5, 222, 266, 280-312, 426, 428, 431, 433, Figs 8.66c-d, 8.82b-c, 10.34, 10.37, 10.45-6, 10.48-71b |
| Ta' Trapna | Żebbuġ | Żebbuġ | 1 | / | / | / | Evans 1971: 168-9, Fig.57, Plate 61 (7,8) |

| Site | | | | | | | |
|---|---|---|---|---|---|---|---|
| Ħal Saflieni Hypogeum | Żebbuġ | Late Ġgantija to Tarxien | / | / | 8 | 15 | Evans 1971: 48, 53, 59-60, 62-3 |
| Xewkija | Għar Dalam | Tarxien (?) | / | / | 1 | / | Evans 1971: 191 |
| Ġgantija | Żebbuġ | Ġgantija | 1 | 4 | / | 3 | Evans 1971: 174-5, 179-81, 184-5, Plate 62 (1-7); NLM, MS 1161: Plates 5, 8-10, 13-17 |
| Tarxien | Żebbuġ | Tarxien | 3 | 2 | / | 39 (excluding the rather aniconic ones from the Cemetery) | Evans 1971: 118, 122, 135-8, 142-5, 151-2, Plates 14 (6), 51 (4-5) |
| Ħaġar Qim | Ġgantija | Ġgantija | 3 | / | 20 | 19 (none from subsidiary buildings) | Evans 1971: 83-5, 87, 89-92, 94, Plate 9 (1) |
| Mnajdra | Żebbuġ | Tarxien | / | 1 | 1 | 11 | Evans 1971: 97, 99, 102-3 |
| Kordin | Żebbuġ | Ġgantija | No amount available | 1 | No amount available | / | Evans 1971: 74, 77-8, 80 |
| Borġ in-Nadur | Tarxien (late?) | Borġ in-Nadur (Bronze Age) | 6 (single pillars only) | / | / | / | Evans 1971: 9-14, 18 |
| Tas-Silġ | Tarxien | Tarxien (for the prehistoric period) | 2 (and other ones in fragments) | / | / | 1 | Missione 1964: 75-6, 179, 191, Plate 30; 1968: 39-40, 78, 118-9, Plate 2 (2-3); 1969: 47; 1970: 55, 98 |

*Figure 22. Table showing elements of aniconic cults in relation to the earliest phases of Maltese prehistoric temples. Elements of figurine-based cults are also drawn in for comparison, particularly in peak phases of the same prehistoric temples' lifetime.*

as they could have equally been a local and independent development) characterised more by the use of stone pillars, cones, and spheres. For a while, the popularity of aniconism seems to have taken over until, perhaps, the late Ġgantija phase when figurines seem to have regained favour in cultic worship, evidently reaching a peak in the Tarxien phase. This would imply that stone pillars, cones, and spheres on the sites discussed may have belonged to earlier phases of their use (most of the sites, in fact, were already in use during the Żebbuġ phase) until the (re-)emergence of more iconic or figurine-based cults from the (late) Ġgantija phase onwards (Figure 22).

Nevertheless, this does not necessarily imply that aniconic cults or traditions were completely diminished and replaced by the more iconic or figurine-based ones but the two types of cults or traditions are more likely to have remained in co-existence to varying extents in different phases and amongst different prehistoric communities on the Maltese islands. That aniconic cults or traditions did not come into oblivion is also confirmed by evidence from later historic periods showing that these cults or traditions survived – even if, perhaps, to lesser degrees – for many other centuries alongside iconic or image-based ones (see below).

## 3.0 Tripillar shrines or altars

At Borġ in-Nadur temple, the presence of betyl stones has already been noted. But this temple has yet more to offer. A semicircular niche (covered by soil and stones when visited by John Evans in 1958) had been earlier cleared by M.A. Murray and was found to contain three uprights (Figure 23. Evans 1971: 12). The shrine was located on the rearmost or western end of Murray's 'apsidal building' (Murray 1925: Plate IX) between Evans' apse 13 and apse 14 (Evans 1971: Plan 1) or Murray's south-west apse and north-west apse respectively (Murray 1925: Plate VIII).

*Figure 23. Three upright stones at Borġ in-Nadur Temple at Birżebbuġa in Malta. Found in a semicircular niche, they may have comprised a tripillar shrine. (Source: Murray 1923: Plate XIX (2))*

The largest of the three upright stones lay somewhat off-centre of the niche and to the south and stood against the niche's back wall and between the other two uprights, one to the north and the other to the south. Yet, as if facing each other, the two flanking uprights stood forward of the central one and at right angles to it, forming a sort of a rectangular space between them. The rock surface of the niche's floor contained an oval hole tapering down conically. This hole was cut to the north of the northern upright stone and contained two implements: one was a flake of chert showing signs of usage along its cutting edge and lay on the bottom of the hole and the other one, which lay on top of the previous, was of black flint and was worked on both sides (Evans 1971: 12; Murray 1923: 22-3, Plates VII, XIX; Murray 1925: Plates VIII-IX).

Another possible set of three uprights may have also existed at the Tas-Silġ sanctuary during its use by the Phoenicians who followed the 'Borġ in-Nadur' people. This possibility is suggested by the presence of a sixth to fifth-century BC altar containing three equidistant sockets evidently meant to hold poles, pillars, or uprights (*Missione 1968*: 118). Altars carrying a similar arrangement – and, thus, could have likewise comprised tripillar altars or shrines – are to be found in nearby Sicily on sites like the sacred area near the beginning of the *agora* at Solunto and the temple of Zeus Meilichios (Figure 24), the temple of Demeter Malophoros, and the *sacello Triolo Nord* (Figure 25) at Selinunte (De Vincenzo 2013: 108 (including Fig.43), 109 (Fig.44), 255 (including Fig.145), 256 (Fig.147), 257 (including Fig.148), 259-62 (including Fig.152), 263; Gaifman 2012: 200-1 (Fig.5.11)). Farther examples – better known as 'tripillar shrines' – come from the 'Fosse Temple' of Lacish in Israel, from Temple 300 at Tell Qasile also in Israel, and from the sanctuary of Kommos in southern Crete (De Vincenzo 2013: 261, 265, Fig.155. For the example from Kommos, see also Brody 1998: 59, Fig.59; Gaifman 2012: 186-8; Prent 2003: 93-4). Comparing the three pillars at the so-called 'Tripillar Shrine' at Kommos with those seen in relief on stelae from Punic tophets (Figure 26. See also example immediately below), Joseph Shaw, the site's excavation director, is of the opinion that the Tripillar Shrine was inspired by Phoenician traditions (Gaifman 2012: 186-8; see also 305).

Tripillars may have represented divine triads. Examples of tripillars from Sardinia seem to have represented Chammanim or (triple) representations of the solar god Ba'al Chammàn. An example is shown in relief on a stela

*Figure 24. Tripillar altar in the temple of Zeus Meilichios at Selinunte, Sicily. (Photo: The Author)*

*Figure 25. Tripillar altar in the sacello Triolo Nord at Selinunte, Sicily. (Photo: The Author)*

*Figure 26. Relief tripillars inside a niche on a stela. The stela comes from the Punic tophet at Tharros in Sardinia and is, now, kept at the Archaeology Museum of Cabras (also in Sardinia). (Photo: The Author)*

from the tophet at Nora (Pesce 2000: 208-9 (Fig.76)) while another example comes from the necropolis at Tharros (Pesce 2000: 219, 221 (Fig.86)). A similar triad is represented in relief on a stela from Lilybaeum (today's Marsala, in Sicily). It carries a votive inscription to Ba'al Chammàn (Pesce 2000: 219).

Tripillars may have also represented minor divine triads. An interesting example comes from early Hellenistic Arkadia, in ancient Greece, in the form of a triple stela (actually, a single stone plaque divided into three equal parts, each topped by a pyramid as if composed of three individual stelai). The Greek word for 'Nymphs' (in the genitive plural) appearing on this monument is distributed evenly with two letters on each stela, ultimately making up the whole word, thus alluding to the homogeneity of this divine triad. Even when in an iconic form, the Nymphs (like the Seasons and the Graces, themselves also minor divinities) often appear in triplicate and in resemblance to each other (Gaifman 2012: 218-22, 309).

On certain occasions, in fact, divine triads could have been represented in iconic form too. In Britain and in certain parts of Germany, for instance, we find the *genii cucullati* wearing hooded cloaks (as their name implies) and represented in triple groups. It has been suggested that they represented forces for good or evil that had to be propitiated (Yeates 2008: 15-16 (including Figs 6-7)). Among the *Hwicce* tribe in Britain, one comes across reliefs of the *Matres* or the consort of Mercury in triple form / representation (Yeates 2008: 144 (including Fig.52)). As he narrates in his *Description of Greece* (8. 25. 3), Pausanias saw three stone images of Demeter, her daughter Kore (or Persephone), and Dionysus in a sanctuary of Eleusinian Demeter that was located on the borders of Thelpusa in Arcadia (Greece). These three fertility-associated deities seem to have enjoyed a communal triadic cult. Closely attached to the socially and economically lower class of the plebs in Rome, a triadic cult of Ceres (the Roman counterpart of Demeter), Liber (the Roman counterpart of Dionysus), and Libera (the Roman counterpart of Persephone) likewise shared a common temple on the Aventine Hill in Rome (Spaeth 1996: xiv-vi, 4-29, 41, 44, 66, 70, 81-99). These three deities were already worshipped together also in Eleusis (in West Attica, Greece), Sicily, and Magna Graecia (Southern Italy) from where their cult reached Rome (Nielsen 2014: 199 (footnote 16)) in 496 BC (Nilsson 1985: 12).

But triple images could have also represented one and the same deity as tripillar arrangements sometimes did and as shown, for example, by the Chammanim mentioned above. A triple image of the goddess Hekate Epipyrgidia, for instance, was set up by Alkamenes in the 5th century BC at the entrance to the Athenian acropolis (Gaifman 2012: 167). In the Italian city of Cosa, evidence from the late Roman period shows Hekate to have been honoured in triple form (Nielsen 2014: 124). This triplicity may have represented three aspects or realms of the goddess (Jung and Kerényi 1969: 112-3. Also, Hesiod, *Theogony* 411ff cited in Jung and Kerényi 1969: 112 (footnote 47)). Earlier, mention has also been made of the consort of Mercury in triple form among the *Hwicce* tribe in Britain (see above).

# 4.0 Betyl amulets?

What appear to have been miniature pillars evidently worn as amulets by deceased individuals were found in tombs at Binġemma, near Rabat (Malta), in 1927. Dated to around the 7th-6th century BC, these presumed miniature betyls were respectively in the form of a Djed pillar and a Ouaz pillar (Gouder 1978: 312 (k-l)). The Djed pillar was not only the symbol of the god Osiris but was also revered as a symbol of survival, stability, and the afterlife. Derived from the form of the lotus flower, the Ouaz pillar was the symbol of rebirth. Both amulets were evidently meant to accompany and provide protection to the deceased in the afterlife.

A miniature pointed pillar (GS2/98) with a perforated end to have it hung round one's neck as a possible amulet (Figure 27) was found on the surface of the forecourt in front of the Ġgantija northern temple (in Xagħra, Gozo) in May 1998. It was found almost on the same spot where a bone bead (GS1/98) had been also found on the surface eleven days earlier (author's unpublished fieldnotes). Both are now on permanent display at the Gozo Archaeology Museum, in the Citadel (Victoria). Although it comes from an insecure context and unless it is a prehistoric version of what follows, the miniature pillar-amulet may have been a Djed pillar of the Phoenician or Punic period (Figure 28) when the mentioned prehistoric Ġgantija temples may have possibly been re-used as was the prehistoric temple at Tas-Silġ (*Missione 1965*: 26; *1966*: 118, 127-8; *1967*: 42; *1970*: 22-3) and as other evidence in the form of a debatable Phoenician inscription on the floor of

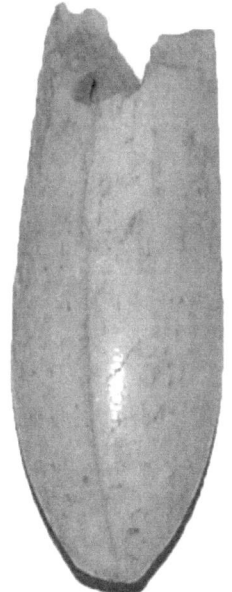

*Figure 27. A possible pillar-amulet. The perforation at its end suggests hanging round one's neck. It was found on the surface of the forecourt in front of the Ġgantija northern temple in Xagħra, Gozo. Now, kept at the Gozo Archaeology Museum in the Citadel, Victoria. (Photo: The Author)*

*Figure 28. Miniature Djed pillars. The examples shown here were meant to be hung as amulets. They are on display at the archaeological museum of the tophet at Sant'Antioco, Sardinia. (Photo: The Author)*

the Ġgantija southern temple (*MAR* 1912-13: 5) and an oriental-style female bust evidently also from Ġgantija (Caruana 1882: 8. See also Gatt 1937: 135-6) may also seem to suggest.

Though not in miniature form or to be worn as amulets, betyls (even if in shapes other than pillars) are also known from funerary contexts elsewhere, evidently also to give protection to the deceased in the afterlife. Apart from the examples mentioned earlier, other examples come from Sardinia: from the necropolis at Tharros (Pesce 2000: 219. See also 6.0 below) and from the tophet at Sulcis (Pesce 2000: Fig.42).

# 5.0 More betyls from Tas-Silġ

Two more possible betyls are evidenced from Tas-Silġ (Figure 21). A presumed small pillar was the object of a dedication to Astarte mentioned in a Punic inscription (see Appendix I), probably of the 2nd-1st century BC, engraved on an architectural element found unstratified in Area 4 at Tas-Silġ (*Missione 1963*: 70, 83-7, 151, Plate 26 (1-2)). If it was itself dedicated to Astarte and represented the same deity, the pillar may have, thus, been equated to statues (including those contemporary with betyls) dedicated to and representing deities or deified imperial family members (as examples, see Ascough, Harland and Kloppenborg 2012: 37 (no 32), 94 (no 147), 139 (no 225)) that (i.e. the statues) shared with betyls the same qualifying criteria, namely religious context, conspicuousness, and special treatment (see 1.2 above). In this way, the presumed pillar might have been an aniconic betyl substituting an image of Astarte to whom it was dedicated and whom it, thus, represented. A cone-shaped pillar with three collars on its top part, perhaps to hold a crown of small leaves, might have been another betyl on the basis of its suggested treatment. Dated not earlier than the 7th century BC, it was also found unstratified in Area 4 (*Missione 1963*: 70, 151).

But a more securely identified betyl is that carved in relief in the middle of a small stone pediment dated to the 3rd century BC-1st century AD. The pediment with the carved betyl found at Tas-Silġ came from division 51 in Area 6 (*Missione 1968*: 40, 78, 119, Plate 5 (3)).

# 6.0 Stone worship at Ras il-Wardija, in Gozo

Evidently in use from the 3rd century BC to the 4th century AD (i.e. from late Punic to late Roman times), the headland sanctuary located at Ras il-Wardija, on the western coast of Gozo, is spread down a natural slope on which eight terraces appear to have been later created, probably for agricultural purposes. The first terrace by the edge of the coastal cliff hosts a small temple which, in its heyday, must have not only dominated the coastal promontory but must have also been visible to sailors navigating along this coastal stretch or approaching either the nearby harbour of Xlendi or the sheltered anchorage at Dwejra. Along with the rest of the sanctuary, this small temple was excavated by the *Missione Archeologica Italiana* in the 1960s (*Missione 1964-7*).

One important find was what the excavators called a 'cippus' (Figure 29). This 'cippus' was found in the space between the external wall of the temple and what is likely to have been a shallow *temenos* wall surrounding the temple. It was also near the temple's entrance and an offering table outside but in front of the said entrance (*Missione 1966*: 104, Plate 75 (3-4)). This stone assumes the shape of a pyramid standing on a base or a pedestal as if to highlight the pyramid's significance. Presently kept in storage at the Gozo Archaeology Museum, it also carries faint traces of thin creamy white plaster with which its surfaces are likely to have been originally covered. Taking into account not only the location where it was found but also its treatment (i.e. plastered surfaces and pedestal support), the stone 'cippus' is very likely to have been a betyl.

A similar betyl comes from a temple site in Nora (in Sardinia) while two others come from Tharros (also in Sardinia), respectively from the small sanctuary at Capo San Marco (Figure 30, left) and from the necropolis. These three pyramidal stones are about 30cm high; almost of the same height as the one from Ras il-Wardija. The example from the Tharros necropolis consists of a pyramid on top of a small square pillar carrying a Punic funerary inscription. While certain scholars do more readily claim these pyramidal betyls to have represented the Carthaginian goddess Tanit, Sabatino Moscati adopts a more cautious approach (Moscati 2005:

*Figure 29. The pyramidal 'cippus' / betyl discovered at Ras il-Wardija. Besides its pyramidal shape, the 'cippus' / betyl also stands on a base or pedestal. (Photo: The Author)*

151-2, 186-7, Figs17, 39; Pesce 2000: 219-21, Fig.85. For the example from the small fifth-century BC sanctuary at Capo San Marco, see also Brody 1998: 59-60 (including note 121), Figs60-1). In fact, pyramidal stones are known to have represented other deities too. In his *Description of Greece*, the second-century AD Greek geographer and traveler Pausanias noted a small pyramidal stone representing Apollo Carinus in the old gymnasium near 'the Gate of the Nymphs' in Megara (1. 44. 2) and another pyramid representing Zeus Meilichius in Sicyon (2. 9. 6), both in ancient Greece. Pyramidal stones of Aphrodite are also known from the Orient (Gaifman 2012: 67 (footnote 67)). Another pyramidal betyl (Figure 30, right) was recently found in the southern necropolis at Tharros (now on permanent display at the Archaeology Museum of Cabras, Sardinia) while more are turning up in excavations conducted by Anna Chiara Fariselli and Carla Del Vais in the same necropolis (Anna Chiara Fariselli personal communication). As the last-mentioned ones come from funerary contexts, they may have served as memorial marks for the dead but could have also been perceived as the abode of the spirits of the dead or their aniconic representation, unless they represented deities protecting the buried deceased (see 1.0 above).

A patch of levelled-out rock floor found almost in the middle of the small temple structure on the first terrace at Ras il-Wardija (*Missione 1967*: 88, Fig.9) could have accommodated the plinth on which the discovered betyl might have stood inside the said structure during the latter's heyday. This might have been around the 3rd century BC which does not only mark the earliest use of the site (see above) but, in a wider Mediterranean context, also witnessed an envisioning of the primeval past marked by the adoption of non-figural monuments for veneration (Gaifman: 2012: 88, 108). As the betyl inside faced the temple structure's entrance, offerings could be made on the offering table facing it outside (Figure 31. See also above). The scene might have been typical of imageless shrines befitting the description – imaginary, yet related to reality – provided by Apollonius Rhodius in his *The Argonautica* (2. 1169-76) with respect to the shrine of Ares by the southern shores of the Black Sea where the Amazons practised stone worship and sacrificed to the stone on an altar that, like the offering table at Ras il-Wardija, faced the stone from outside the temple (Gaifman 2012: 110-2; see also 305).

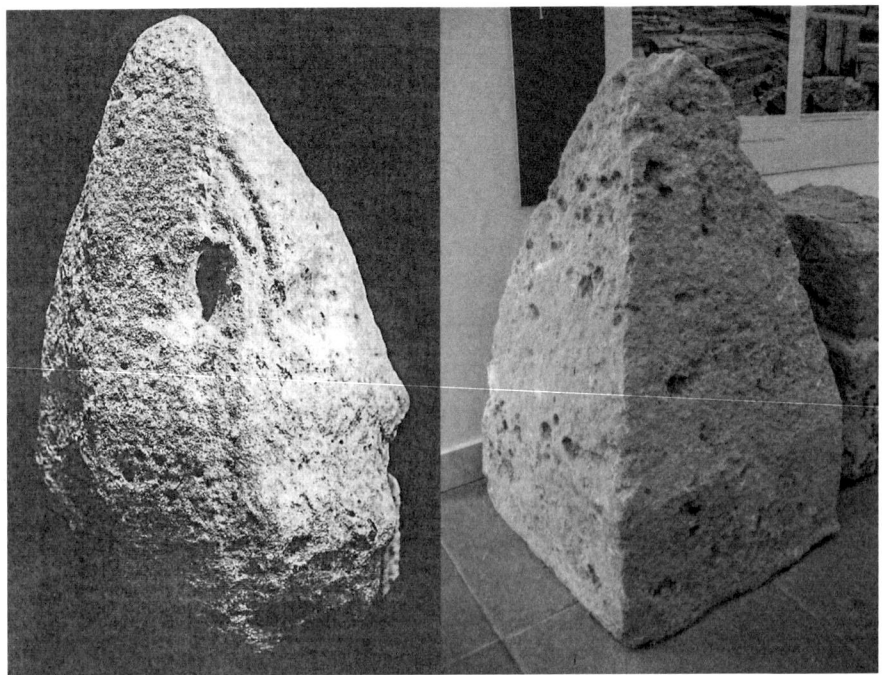

*Figure 30. A pyramidal stone from the small sanctuary at Capo San Marco (left) and a pyramidal betyl from Tharros' southern necropolis, Sardinia (right). The latter is on permanent display at the Archaeology Museum of Cabras, also in Sardinia. (Left photo source: Pesce 2000: 220 (Fig.85); Right photo: The Author)*

When the temple structure (or the betyl itself) at Ras il-Wardija went out of use, the betyl appears to have been removed from its central place but was maintained within the sacred precinct and close to the offering table perhaps on account of its sacred character (as in Glinister 2000: 56-60, 67-70). The discovery of a coin (undecipherable) and part of a small metal chain in the same area where the betyl was found (*Missione 1966*: 107) may suggest that, along with the betyl, these may have formed a structured deposit perhaps marking the termination of the ritual use of the betyl or even of the temple itself (as in Glinister 2000: 69-70). A similar chain fragment made of gold was found at Tas-Silġ sanctuary in Malta (*Missione 1965*: 37, Plate 24 (4)).

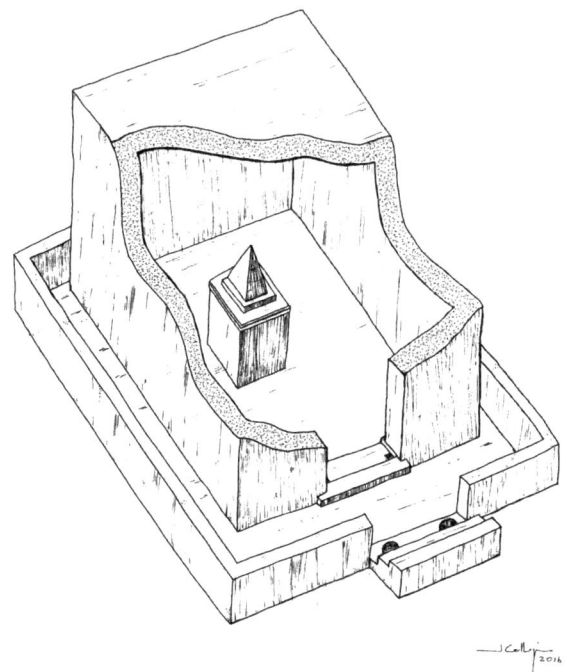

*Figure 31. An artist's impression of the temple on the first terrace at Ras il-Wardija, in Gozo. It includes a cut-out view showing the interior where the pyramidal betyl might have received worship. (Drawing: Joseph Calleja)*

Another possible betyl (Figure 32) might have been a stone in the shape of a small column of a height ranging from 23cm to 25.5cm. Its surface looks to be rendered in the form of a spiral (*Missione 1965*: 140, Plate 102 (3)). Its betylic nature seems to be suggested not only by its surface treatment but also by the context in which it was found.

A set of two rock-cut conical cavities following an arrangement very similar to that of the offering table mentioned above were found beyond and in front of the entrance to the cave on the fifth terrace. They lay at an intersection of passages and rock-cut 'benches' which they formed part of. It appears that a subsequent need for a further extension of the rock-cut 'bench' (perhaps to create more space) necessitated the insertion of two stone blocks of different sizes to create a continuous 'bench' on the side of the same passage, hiding the two conical cavities permanently from view and, at the same time, creating what the excavators termed 'a basin' with the two conical cavities consequently finding themselves on its bottom (Missione 1964: 171-2, Fig.12, Plates 76-8; 1965: 131, Fig.8, Plates 86, 90 (1)-1 (1), 94 (3), 100 (2)). The space within the basin and above the two conical cavities yielded the above-mentioned small stone column that seems to have been deliberately deposited above the two conical cavities with which it might have been previously closely associated. In fact, along with a ceramic sherd found within the same infilling material (Missione 1965: 140, Fig.8, Plates 86, 91 (2), 94 (3), 102 (3)), the small stone column may have formed a structured deposit marking the termination of the ritual use of both presumed offering table and associated stone column.

This seems, therefore, to confirm that the pair of two conical cavities comprised an offering table behind which might have stood the stone column as a betyl or an aniconic representation of a deity to whom offerings were made on the offering table (Figure 33). When both offering table and stone column / betyl went out of use and their ritual use was terminated, the stone column / betyl was deposited over the offering table and everything was covered over, both to maintain the sacred objects within the sacred precinct and to enable the continuation of the rock-cut bench flanking the passage.

Two very schematic cruciform figures (besides another one – possibly, two – in 'flying' attitude) are engraved on the interior of the man-made cave on the fifth terrace (Missione 1964: 169, Plate 75 (1); 1965: 126-7, Plate 83). One such deeply-engraved cruciform figure on the back-wall of one of the niches of the said cave (Figure 34) is sometimes claimed to be a representation of Tanit. But although this cruciform figure is semi-anthropomorphic like the common schematic symbol of Tanit consisting of a triangle or a betyl with outstretched arms and head, it lacks any secure attributes of this goddess while it could have also been made in later times of the sanctuary's lifetime. On the other hand, very similar cruciform figures appear on a stela from the Punic tophet at Nora, in Sardinia and on another stela from the Punic tophet at Sulcis (Sant' Antioco), also in Sardinia. These schematic

*Figure 32. Small 'column' betyl with its surface rendered in the form of a spiral. It was found beyond and in front of the entrance to the cave on the fifth terrace at Ras il-Wardija, in Gozo. (Photo: The Author)*

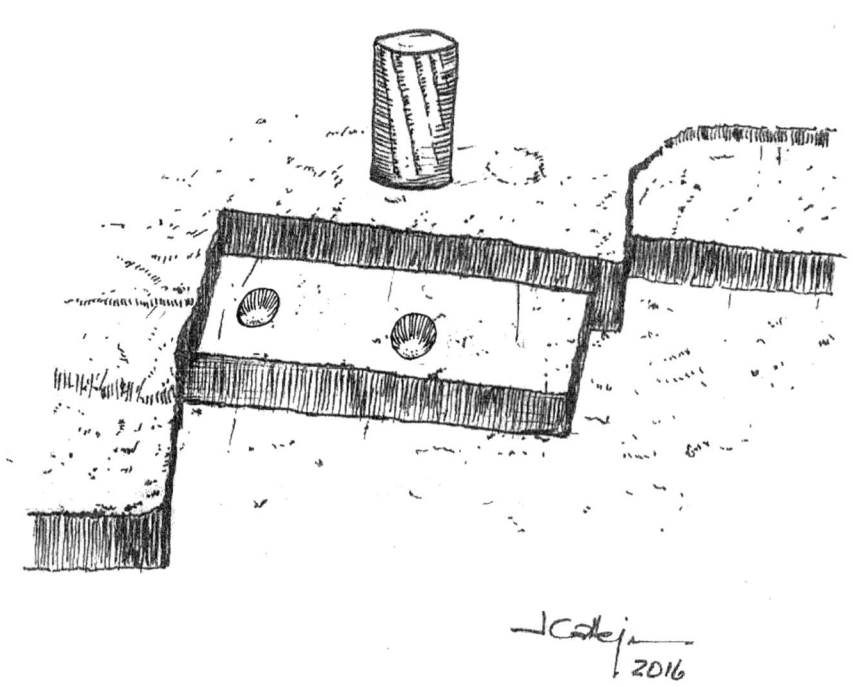

*Figure 33. An artist's impression of the 'column' betyl standing behind the two conical cavities on top of which it was found. The two conical cavities might have been an offering table from where, standing behind, the betyl could have received offerings. (Drawing: Joseph Calleja)*

cruciform figures are interpreted by Sabatino Moscati (2005: 212 (Fig.62)-3, 218 (Fig.69)-9) as possibly representing a transitional stage in the evolution from aniconism to iconism (or anthropomorphism) in the form of a betyl which is humanised with the addition of two outstretched arms (see also Pesce 2000: 196). The schematic cruciform figures at Ras il-Wardija may, perhaps, be also thought of as being an imitation of cruciform herms (Figure 35) which, in their semi-figural form (see Gaifman 2012: 36, 234-8. Also 1.0 above), may likewise represent a transitional stage in the evolution from aniconism to iconism (see Gaifman 2012: 232-4. Also 1.0 above). If the schematic cruciform figures at Ras il-Wardija did indeed represent such a transitional stage (without, however, excluding alternative explanations), it may, therefore, be suggested that these semi-anthropomorphic figures post-date the pyramidal betyl and, presumably, also the small temple on the

*Figure 34. Figure with outstretched hands in a niche inside the cave at Ras il-Wardija, in Gozo. This cruciform and semi-anthropomorphic figure may have represented a transitional stage in the evolution from aniconism to iconism. (Source: MISSIONE 1965: Plate 83 (3))*

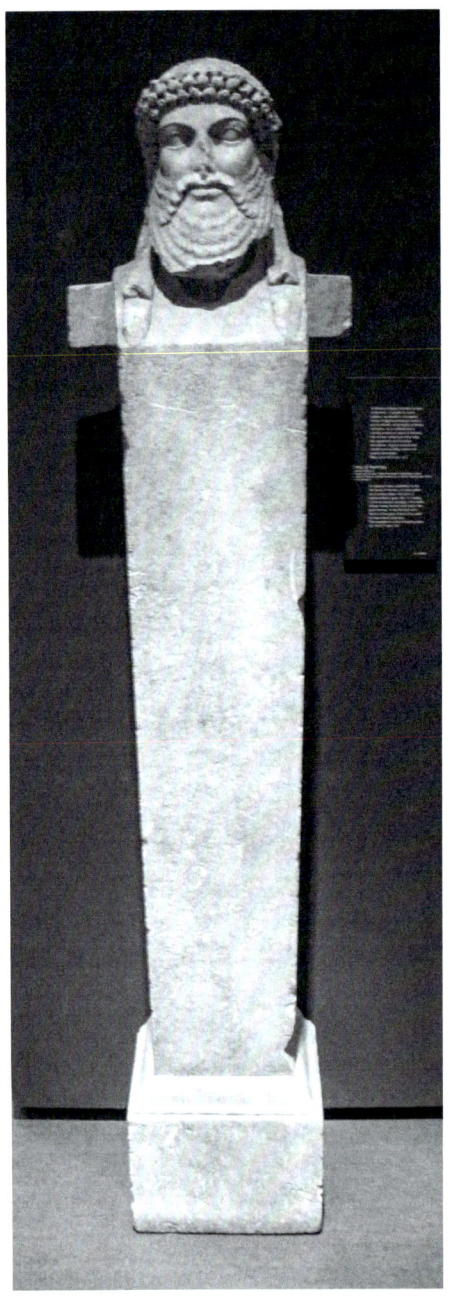

first terrace that accommodated it as well as the small 'column' betyl found in front of the cave on the mentioned fifth terrace. They might have been carved, in fact, in a later stage of their hosting cave's lifetime.

It is unclear whether the presumed structured deposition of both pyramidal betyl and 'column' betyl marked the termination of the sanctuary's use or solely the termination (or replacement) of the aniconic cults themselves. But as no figurines or figurine fragments are reported to have been found at the Ras il-Wardija sanctuary complex (including the temple structure on the first terrace), it may be suggested that the cult at Ras il-Wardija remained largely aniconic throughout.

*Figure 35. A cruciform herm of the god Hermes. It is to be found at the Museo Nazionale Romano Palazzo Massimo, Rome. (Photo: The Author)*

# 7.0 A pair of 'twin' betyls

It has already been shown in 1.2 above that betyls may also occur in pairs or as twins. The earliest example on the Maltese islands may, perhaps, come again from Tas-Silġ sanctuary in the area of Marsaxlokk. The two betyls in question are to be found respectively in Areas 3 and 6 of the sanctuary complex (see 2.0 above). Michelangelo Cagiano de Azevedo has identified in the prehistoric betyl located in the southern area (Area 3) the twin of the other prehistoric one located next to a stone basin in the northern area (Area 6) (*Missione 1970*: 98).

From later times, two identical marble cippi (Figure 36) are claimed by Ciantar (1772: 527-8, 561, Plate X) to have been discovered (or re-discovered?) together and with their presumably tapering apex broken and missing on Corradino Hill, overlooking the Grand Harbour in Malta. Their true original provenance, however, is still debatable but there seems to be a general agreement on the fact that they were found together (Mercieca 2014: 36-7, Figs4-5).

With its lower part decorated with low reliefs of acanthus foliage alternating with lotus buds, each one of these cippi assumes a vertical ovoid profile almost looking like a flowering bud itself, and stands on a pedestal. Their respective – and likewise identical – pedestals carry a mutually similar bilingual inscription in Punic and Greek (*CIS*, I, 122 a, b), recording an unspecified offering or dedication made to Melqart (whose name appears in the main Punic inscription) or to his Greek equivalent Heracles (whose name appears in the Greek version). The donors' names are also given in both Punic and Greek versions in the respective inscriptions (see Appendix II). These identical cippi with their inscribed pedestals are dated to the 2nd century BC (Bonanno (with Cilia) 2005: 121, 151). One is still in Malta, at the National Museum of Archaeology in Valletta, while the other one is now in the Louvre Museum in Paris after it had been donated to King Louis XVI of France in 1780.

A seemingly similar Punic cippus (Figure 37) surfaced (albeit out of context) in 1983 from the area of Santa Gilla in Cagliari, Sardinia, and is now on display in the *Museo Archeologico Nazionale* of Cagliari (Amadasi Guzzo

*Figure 36. The two identical marble cippi each carrying a bilingual inscription in Punic and Greek. The inscriptions record an unspecified offering or dedication to Melqart / Heracles. The cippus on the left is still in Malta and is kept at the National Museum of Archaeology in Valletta while the one on the right is in the Louvre Museum in Paris, France. (Photograph © Daniel Cilia)*

2002: 173, 176 (note 1); Minoja, Cossu and Migaleddu 2012: 86). Like the Maltese examples, this marble cippus also assumes a vertical ovoid profile. Although it lacks any base in its present state, a plug-like arrangement on its present lowermost part seems to suggest that this fitted on a base or pedestal of some sort (see Amadasi Guzzo 2002: 173, 178 (Tav. I); Minoja, Cossu and Migaleddu 2012: 86) as the Maltese examples do. The topmost part is only partially and laterally broken with its remaining flat top surface suggesting no upward extension. This gives it a total height of 96cm, albeit without the presumed additional base. The topmost part carries a frieze of palmette motifs beneath which there is a Punic inscription recording the dedication of the same cippus (referred to as consisting of a tall stone) to Melqart of Tyre by Hanno, son of Bod'aštart, son of 'Abdmilkot, son of Šapot (see Appendix III). On the basis of the characteristics betrayed by this inscription, the cippus is dated to the period between the end of the 4th and the first half of the 3rd century BC (Amadasi Guzzo 2002: 173-5, 178 (Tav. I)-179 (Tav. II); Minoja, Cossu, and Migaleddu 2012: 86). Besides carrying a dedication to the same deity (i.e. Melqart of Tyre) as that on the Maltese cippi, the inscription also adopts a formulaic pattern (1st: dedicatee, 2nd: offering / dedication, 3rd: dedicator/s, 4th: genealogy of the dedicator/s) similar to that adopted in the Punic inscriptions on the two Maltese cippi and common in Punic dedicatory inscriptions (Amadasi Guzzo 2002: 174-6 (note 14); Minoja, Cossu, and Migaleddu 2012: 86).

Two much closer examples to the Maltese ones are, in fact, provided by two neo-Punic inscriptions on stelae in spite of the interchangeable positions of certain textual parts. One is from Maktar (in Tunisia), carrying a dedication to Baal by a certain Dabar for having heard his voice and blessed him. The other (now, in the British Museum) is unprovenanced and carries a dedication to Baal by a certain Balonag for having heard her voice and blessed her. Both inscriptions carry the genealogy of the respective dedicators (Moore 2000: 133-4). As in the Maltese examples, the offering / dedication is not mentioned but might have possibly been the stelae themselves.

Unfortunately, the precise context in which the two Maltese cippi were found is unknown. Although they are elsewhere claimed to have been candelabra supporting a receptacle containing fire or burnt incense or a

*Figure 37. A marble cippus from the area of Santa Gilla in Cagliari, Sardinia. It carries a Punic inscription recording the dedication of the same cippus to Melqart of Tyre. The cippus is kept in the Museo Archeologico Nazionale of Cagliari. (Source: Amadasi Guzzo 2002: 178 (Tav.I))*

round shelf holding a lamp (Bonanno (with Cilia) 2005: 153), their treatment (i.e. their foliage decoration and, especially, their pedestal support with an inscribed dedication) along with the fact that they were found together and constitute a pair like those betyls that are also sometimes found in pairs (see 1.2 above) may suggest that they were, more probably, a pair of betyls.

More importantly, as the offering or dedication recorded in each inscription beneath the respective 'cippi' / betyls is referred to but not specified (in spite of the fact that each inscription is complete), it seems logical to suggest that the 'cippi' / betyls themselves formed the object of dedication to Melqart / Heracles as was clearly the case with the similar Cagliari example. Their stylistic similarity to that of the Cagliari example together with the formulaic similarity of their respective inscriptions to that on the same Cagliari example (which is known to have been itself the object of dedication) may lend further support to this suggestion. The same opinion is expressed by Amadasi Guzzo (2002: 175).

That stones in the form of cippi (or even stelae) could be dedicated to deities is also demonstrated by further examples from Sardinia. Besides the Cagliari example mentioned immediately above, a cippus made of trachyte (an igneous volcanic rock) in the form of an upward-tapering parallelepiped block from the tophet area at Sant' Antioco (ancient Sulcis) was dedicated to Baal Hammon as we learn from the inscription carried by the same cippus (Minoja, Cossu and Migaleddu 2012: 45). Two sets of twin cippi and twin stelae evidently originating from the *isola di San Pietro* were both dedicated to Baalshamim. These do no longer survive but are known from an inscription referring to their dedication to Baalshamim and which is carried on what appears to be their surviving common stone base (Minoja, Cossu and Migaleddu 2012: 82). What is particularly more interesting about these twin cippi and twin stelae is their dual form and their dedication to a common deity which makes them all the more similar to the Maltese twin cippi (see below).

As an epitome of visual culture (a statue) complemented by epigraphy (a dedicatory inscription), dedicated statues (including those contemporary with betyls) with the relative dedicatory inscription beneath often represented the deities or deified imperial family members to whom the dedication was made (as examples, see Ascough, Harland and Kloppenborg 2012: 37 (no 32), 94 (no 147), 139 (no 225)). The suggested occurrence whereby our 'cippi' / betyls with their relative dedicatory inscription beneath might have been themselves the object of dedication might, thus, equate them (as well as the Cagliari and the other Sardinian examples) to dedicated statues with their likewise relative dedicatory inscription beneath which, like betyls, also often come from religious contexts, are conspicuous, and receive special treatment (see 1.2 above). A similar example might have been the presumed pillar / betyl dedicated to Astarte and found at Tas-Silġ (see 5.0 above). Therefore, in the Maltese case under review where the dedication is directed to Melqart / Heracles according to the relative dedicatory inscription beneath each 'cippus', each of the two 'cippi' might have played the role of an aniconic betyl substituting an image or statue of Melqart / Heracles whom it (i.e. each 'cippus' / betyl), thus, represented and to whom it was also dedicated (see also Falsone 1993: 246). The same also applies in respect of the Cagliari and the other Sardinian examples which, likewise, might have been aniconic betyls that were not only dedicated to but also substituted an image of and represented Melqart in the case of the Cagliari example and respectively Baal Hammon and Baalshamim in the case of the other two Sardinian examples.

Consequently, while it might have been reminiscent of the Egyptian incorporation of foliage (particularly acanthus) in column drums (as in Gaifman 2012: 280-1), the resemblance of our presumed betyls to a flowering bud might have emphasised the fertility aspect of the deity or, else, as the lotus flower is a symbol of rebirth, the presumed Maltese betyls' seemingly more specific resemblance to a lotus flower bud (which they also happen to carry in low relief) might have, in this case, highlighted Heracles' mythical rebirth / ἔγερσιζ (Jane L. Ainsworth personal communication). In fact, an association of a lotus flower with Heracles indicating his mythical rebirth might be analogous to an association of a lotus flower with a deceased person (in a funerary context) to indicate his rebirth to a new life following death. This seems to be the meaning conveyed by the depiction of a lotus flower next to a deceased person's name as they appear, for instance, on a gold ring found in a funerary context (tomb XXVI) in the necropolis of Nora, in Sardinia (Minoja, Cossu and Migaleddu 2012: 69).

However, also in emphasis on the fertility aspect of the deity, the presumed betyls under review might also be perceived as a representation of the deity emerging or springing up from a bud. Thus seem to indicate, for instance, betyl representations of Apollon Agyieus that often stand on a base and are likewise decorated with acanthus foliage, sometimes also alternating with what appear to be lotus buds, on their lowermost part in a manner very similar to that of the Maltese examples (see examples in *LIMC* II/1: 328-30 (10, 15-16, 21, 27; II/2: 280 (10), 281 (15-16, 21), 283 (27)). A Roman example of the Claudian period, now in the *Museo Civico* of Padova (Italy), even carries a further decorative band with foliage and a birds' nest midway up along its height (Figure 38). The contents of an inscription incorporated in the decorative band indicate that the betyl comes from a funerary context (*LIMC* II/1: 330 (27); II/2: 283 (27)). If taken as a symbol of birth / rebirth, the birds' nest may further confirm the fertility aspect of the deity represented by the betyl in question while, in respect of the buried deceased, it may have signified rebirth. Betyls representing deities are also known from funerary contexts where the represented deities might have provided protection to the buried deceased (see 6.0 above) or, else, secured rebirth to the deceased as it seems to have been in this case. The topmost parts of many of the Apollon Agyieus betyls have mushroom-shaped terminals with a cone-shaped finial on the very top (as examples, see *LIMC* II/1: 329 (15-16, 21); II/2: 281 (15-16, 21)). It is unclear whether the broken apex of the presumed Maltese twin betyls had a similar terminal or not.

Moreover, the duality of these presumed (Maltese) twin betyls may have represented the dual or twin columnar form of Melqart / Heracles. Dual or twin columnar forms (like the above example from the *isola di San Pietro*, in Sardinia) are known to have been attributed to deities (including Melqart at Gades, in southern Spain) elsewhere too (Evans 1901: 133, 144-5).

The similar mutilation of their apex suffered by both of the presumed (Maltese) betyls might suggest a deliberate mutilation. This suggested deliberate mutilation might have taken place as part of a desacralisation exercise (perhaps, involving also deposition) and, possibly, also to prevent their re-use when their ritual use was terminated. Similarly deliberate mutilations were also, sometimes, suffered by statues / statuettes (in ritual contexts) for similar reasons.

*Figure 38. A betyl representation of Apollon Agyieus decorated with acanthus foliage on its lowermost part. As indicated by an inscription it carries, it comes from a funerary context. This Roman betyl dates to the Claudian period and is now kept in the Museo Civico of Padova, in Italy. (Source: LIMC II/2: 283 (Plate 27))*

# 8.0 A gilded betyl in the temple of Proserpina at Mtarfa

A temple dedicated to the goddess Proserpina is known by way of a commemorative inscription (Figure 39) found on Mtarfa hill (in Malta) in 1613 (Abela 1647: 209). Although found in fragments (a number of which also went missing), the entire inscribed text was later reconstructed with the aid of earlier sources (Mercieca 2014: 35-9, Figs1, 3).

*Figure 39. The inscription CIL, X, 7494 recording repairs and renovation works to an old temple of Proserpina by Chrestion, the procurator of the Maltese islands. It was found in fragments on Mtarfa hill, in Malta, in 1613. (Photograph © Daniel Cilia)*

This inscription (*CIL*, X, 7494) records repairs and renovation works to an old rural temple dedicated to Proserpina that seems to have stood on Mtarfa hill (where the inscription was found) outside the ancient urban centre and town of *Melite* (Figure 40). The repairs and renovation works were carried out by a certain Chrestion, described in the mentioned inscription as an *Augusti libertus* and *procurator* of the islands of Malta and Gozo. The inscription also specifies the temple components that were repaired or renovated because of their old age and, among these, what is most relevant for the purpose of this study is the *pila* which Chrestion gilded (see Appendix IV).

It was not unusual for statues (cultic or otherwise) to be gilded. Such instances are sometimes recorded both in literature (e.g. the gilded statue of Artemis in the market-place at Sicyon, in ancient Greece, and the gilded image (except face, hand, and feet) of Athena in her temple on top of one of the citadels in

*Figure 40. Mtarfa hill (in Malta) outside the ancient urban centre and town of Melite. On the basis of inscription CIL, X, 7494 found there, the hill seems to have been the place where an old temple of Proserpina once stood. The photograph reproduced here shows British military barracks on the hill and was taken before 1918. (Photo: Author's collection)*

Megara, also in ancient Greece, as recorded by Pausanias in his *Description of Greece* (2. 9. 6 and 1. 42. 4 respectively)) and also in inscriptions (e.g. *CIL*, XIV, 375 from Ostia, in Italy and HD015040 from Ephesus, in Turkey). Nevertheless, in the Maltese temple of Proserpina, a *pila* received the same treatment normally accorded to statues. This treatment would, thus, suggest that the importance attached to the *pila* might have equated it with a statue. So much so, this *pila* not only warranted the above-mentioned treatment but also warranted specific mention in the inscription. It was not an ordinary *pila*.

The word '*pila*' has more than one meaning. It could be a mortar which, however, is not expected to be gilded as this *pila* was and is more to be found in domestic, agricultural, or industrial contexts. A *pila* could be also a sun-dial but, on account of the expected rural character of Proserpina's temple on Mtarfa hill and its presumed lack of any high degree of monumentality involving obelisks or sun-dials, this meaning is also unlikely to fit this temple's context. Not alien to this same context, however, a *pila* could be also either a pillar or a sphere. But as a pillar, the *pila* under review is unlikely to have served as a base for a statue for one can hardly expect such treatment (mentioned above) to be accorded to the base at the expense or to the exclusion of the statue. Moreover, in contrast with the *pila* (and the other temple components), no mention is made of a statue had there been any. One would wonder how possible it might have been for a statue to be the only component in a temple to be left unrestored and, thus, unmentioned. On the other hand, both pillar and sphere shapes are often assumed by betyls (see 1.2 above). As it may have been equated with a statue (see above) for which it may have, thus, served as a substitute, the *pila* under review – whether it was a pillar or a sphere – is likely to have been actually an aniconic betyl substituting an image of Proserpina whom it (i.e the *pila* / betyl), therefore, represented.

A somewhat close analogy can, perhaps, be provided by the gilded Ark of the Covenant (itself an aniconic object) that, for the ancient Israelites, signified divine presence and, like cult statues in different contexts, stood inside the temple or its equivalent (Exodus 25: 10-22; 37: 1-9). An even closer analogy may be provided by the bronze gilded (or covered) log of Dionysus Cadmus that was to be found on the Theban acropolis and was said to have fallen from the sky (Pausanias, *Description of Greece* 9. 12. 3-4). Adorned with bronze, this heavenly piece of wood / wooden column was named as the god himself (Gaifman 2012: 73-4, 129; Kerényi 1976: 195-6).

But golden pillars presumably also signifying divine presence are known too. Quoting Menander, Flavius Josephus in his *Against Apion* (1. 18. 118) and in his *Jewish Antiquities* (8. 5. 3) narrates that Eiromos / Hirom, king of Phoenician Tyre, dedicated the golden pillar ('*columna aurea*') in the temple of Jupiter, evidently in an act synonymous to that of the dedication of statues (see 7.0 above) and, thus, this golden pillar might have, in fact, substituted a statue whereby it (i.e. the pillar), therefore, acted as a betyl. Mention of this same golden pillar at Tyre is also made by Eusebius in his *Preparation for the Gospel* (9. 34. 18-19), referring to it as a gift to the king of Tyre by the Israelite king Solomon. Another golden column ('*columna aurea*') which might have likewise been a betyl is the one which, according to Coelius cited by Cicero in his *On Divination* (1. 24. 48), Hannibal wished to carry off from Juno's temple at Lacinium (modern Capo delle Colonne) in Calabria, South Italy (see also Busuttil 2015: 63 (endnote 13)).

The presence of *hederae distinguentes* (ivy leaf motifs) flanking the final word in our commemorative inscription already places the inscription in the Roman imperial period (Calabi Limentani 1968: 149) but perhaps not earlier than the second half of the 2nd century AD when *hederae distinguentes* became common. At Rome, the use of *hederae distinguentes* may have had its origins during the Trajanic period (AD 98-117) although, elsewhere in the empire, it was found even earlier. However, it became common during the second half of the 2nd century AD (Cooley 2012: 432). In the same inscription, Chrestion is referred to as *Augusti libertus*, indicating that Chrestion was a freedman of the emperor (who is not mentioned by name but simply referred to as *Augustus*: a title attributed to all Roman emperors). The appellation *Augusti libertus* started to be used as from the time of the Flavian dynasty (AD 69-96) (Cooley 2012: 411). This provides a *terminus post quem* for the renovations and for the inscription which must have been set up shortly afterwards to commemorate the said renovations. Therefore, the repairs and renovations (including the gilding of the *pila* / betyl) were not carried out before *c*. AD 69; perhaps not even before the second half of the 2nd century AD in view of what has been said above. However, the renovated temple was older.

This seems to imply that the temple in honour of Proserpina had been erected long before the second half of the 1st century AD; perhaps, centuries earlier. But the cult (of Proserpina) appears to have retained its aniconic character down to later times. This may explain the survival of an archaic representation (i.e. in the form of a *pila* / betyl) of Proserpina in Roman imperial times.

Similar examples of long-surviving aniconic cults are known from elsewhere too. For instance, the aniconic cult of Aphrodite at Paphos in Cyprus is known to have survived well into Roman times. The goddess' cone-shaped betyl is shown on Roman coinage of Paphos from the age of Augustus (1st century AD) to the reign of Caracalla (late 2nd-early 3rd century AD) (Budin 2014: 204 (Fig.10)-5; Gaifman 2012: 113-4, 170-5 (including Figs4.20-3), 309) while the Roman historian Tacitus (*c.* AD 56-117) mentions it in association with the goddess (see also 1.3 above) in his *The Histories* (2. 3 quoted in Budin 2014: 205) written around AD 100-10. Likewise, the temple of Emesa (in Syria) dedicated to El-Gabal (*God of the Mountain*), the Syrian sun god, is shown with the betyl of the god on the reverse of a bronze coin struck by the third-century AD usurper Uranius Antoninus, probably in AD 254 (Gaifman 2012: 176; http://en.wikipedia.org/wiki/Royal_family_of_Emesa. Accessed: 1-3-2015). Another example also showing the survival of an aniconic cult down to, at least, the early 3rd century AD is a coin of emperor

*Figure 41. A coin from Byblos showing a betyl in the middle of a sacred enclosure of an old shrine evidently dedicated to Hera. Dated to the early 3rd century AD, this coin gives testimony to the survival of aniconic cults in Roman imperial times. (Source: Moscati 1973: 76 (Fig.4))*

Macrinus (AD 217-18) from the Phoenician city of Byblos (Figure 41. Moscati 1973: 76-7, Fig.4). A betyl is shown in the middle of a colonnaded sacred enclosure forming part of a shrine that was already old (like the temple of Proserpina in Malta). The shrine was evidently dedicated to the goddess Hera whose name together with her 'star' symbol (as a celestial deity) appear in association with the shrine. The betyl, therefore, is presumed to have represented the same goddess.

Writing in the 2nd century AD, Pausanias attests in his *Description of Greece* (7. 22. 4) that, in his time, stones were still venerated by the Greeks at Pharae as "locally meaningful and highly cherished objects" (Gaifman 2012: 118 (including footnote 172)). Then, as late as the 4th century AD, Mithraic stone worship earned the criticism of the early Christian writer Firmicus Maternus in his *The Error of the Pagan Religions* (20. 1. See also Meyer 1999: 207-8).

# 9.0 Conclusion

Figurative representation is the earliest form of attested representation on the Maltese islands, going back to the prehistoric Red Skorba phase (4,400-4,100 BC) of the Neolithic period in Malta. Aniconism made its first evident appearance during the subsequent Żebbuġ phase (4,100-3,700 BC), albeit in the form of crudely anthropomorphised pillars. For a while, it seems to have enjoyed most popularity. But, by the late Ġgantija phase (3,600-3,200 BC), figurative representation regained favour (having already preceded aniconism during the earlier Red Skorba phase; perhaps, it may have never been completely obliterated). However, both types of representation continued to co-exist to varying degrees in different phases and periods down to, at least, the second half of the 1st century AD. A typical example of this continuity is, perhaps, best provided at Tas-Silġ multi-period religious site where, on one and the same site, one finds at least two prehistoric betyls (*Missione 1967*: 39-40, 78, 118-9, Plate 2 (2-3); *1970*: 55), a tripillar altar of the early historic / Phoenician period (*Missione 1968*: 118), and a relief betyl of the 3rd century BC-1st century AD (*Missione 1968*: 40, 78, 119, (Plate 5 (3)) alongside figurative images of both prehistoric (*Missione 1964*: 75-6, 179, 191, Plate 30) and historic periods (*Missione 1964*: 43, 47, 58, 77-8, Plates 34, 47 (1,3); *1965*: 32, 35-7, 42, Plates 12, 15 (3-4), 17-8, 20 (2), 23 (1)-4 (5); *1967*: 23, Plate 14 (4-5); *1968*: 30-2, 34, 38, 46, Plate 7; *1969*: 60).

While Maltese aniconism may have equally been a local and independent development, the fact that it (i.e. aniconism) is typically an eastern phenomenon may also imply that the Żebbuġ phase people evidently responsible for its introduction on the Maltese islands may have been of eastern extraction. The survival of the same phenomenon until, at least, the second half of the 1st century AD may also be explained in the light of the survival, in Roman Malta, of Phoenician / Punic traditions that, on account of their eastern origins, were familiar with the phenomenon. The same, in fact, happened in eastern cities (like the Syrian Emesa and the Phoenician Byblos mentioned in 8.0 above) in Roman times as shown by their coinage of that period.

# Appendix I

A Punic inscription on an architectural element. Tas-Silġ (Malta). Probably, 2nd-1st century BC.

**Translation** (after Garbini in *MISSIONE 1963*: 86):

'pṣ-yaton has dedicated
a small pillar (?) to Lady
Astarte.

# Appendix II

**CIS, I, 122 a, b**

Bilingual inscription in Punic and Greek on each of two twin marble betyls. Corradino (Malta). 2nd century BC.

**Translation** (Bonanno (with Cilia) 2005: 153):

**Punic inscription:**

To our lord Melqart, lord of Tyre, offering by your servant Abdosir and his brother Osirxamar, sons of Osirxamar, son Of Abdosir, for hearing their voice; let him bless them.

**Greek version:**

Dionysios and Sarapion, sons of Sarapion, to Tyrian Herakles, lord of that city.

# Appendix III

A Punic inscription on a marble betyl.
Santa Gilla, Cagliari (Sardinia). Between the end of the 4th and the first half of the 3rd century BC.

**Translation** (after Amadasi Guzzo 2002: 173):

To the lord Melqart on (of?) Tyre.
A tall stone "cippus" which was
dedicated by Hanno, son of Bod'aštart,
son of 'Abdmilkot, son of Šapot.

# Appendix IV

**CIL, X, 7494**

Fragmented but reconstructed Roman inscription.
Mtarfa (Malta). After *c.* AD 69.

**Text:**

1. CHRE[STION AVG(VSTI) L(I)B(ERTVS)] PROC(VRATOR)
2. INSV[LARVM MELIT(AE) ET] GAVL(I)
3. COLVMNA[S CVM] FASTI[GIIS
4. ET PA]RIETI[BVS TEM]PLI [DEAE
5. PROSERPINAE VETVSTATE
6. RVINAM INMINEN]TI[S
7. ---- RES]
8. TITVI[T] SI[MVL ET PILA]M
9. [INAVRAVIT]

**Translation:**

Chrestion, freedman of Augustus and *procurator* of the islands of Malta and Gozo, repaired the columns together with the roof pediments and walls of the temple of the goddess Proserpina which were about time to collapse because of their old age, and at the same time he gilded the pillar / sphere.

# Bibliography

## Abbreviated titles

| | |
|---|---|
| CIL | *Corpus Inscriptionum Latinarum* (Berlin, 1853- ). |
| CIS | *Corpus Inscriptionum Semiticarum* (Paris, 1881-1961). |
| HD | *Heidelberg (Epigraphic) Database* (http://edh-www.adw.uni-heidelberg.de/edh/inschrift/HD015040? Accessed: 15-3-2015). |
| LIMC | *Lexicon Iconographicum Mythologiae Classicae* (Zurich and Munich, 1981-2009). |
| MAR | *Museums Annual Report* (Malta, 1905-2002). |
| MISSIONE | *Missione Archeologica Italiana a Malta. Rapporto Preliminare della Campagna 1963-70* (Roma, 1964-73). |
| MS | *Manuscript* |
| NLM | *National Library of Malta* |

## Ancient sources

| | |
|---|---|
| Apollonius Rhodius | *The Argonautica* |
| Cicero | *On Divination* |
| Clement of Alexandria | *Exhortation to the Greeks* |
| Eusebius | *Preparation for the Gospel* |
| Exodus | (Biblical Old Testament book of) |
| Firmicus Maternus | *The Error of the Pagan Religions* |
| Flavius Josephus | *Against Apion* |
| Flavius Josephus | *Jewish Antiquities* |
| Genesis | (Biblical Old Testament book of) |
| Hesiod | *Theogony* |
| Hosea | (Biblical Old Testament book of) |
| Pausanias | *Description of Greece* |
| Pliny the Elder | *The Natural History* |
| Tacitus | *The Histories* |

## Manuscripts

NLM, MS 1161 (Series of Twenty-one coloured Drawings of the Druidical Remains discovered in the Island of Gozo near Malta. Taken on the spot in the year 1820 by C. de Brochtorff. London, South Lambeth, June 1849).

## Digital sources

http://edh-www.adw.uni-heidelberg.de/edh/inschrift/HD015040?
http://en.wikipedia.org/wiki/Royal_family_of_Emesa.
www.geocities.ws/maltashells/NatHist.html.

## Published works

Abela, G. F. 1647. *Della Descrittione di Malta isola nel mare Siciliano con le sue Antichita', ed altre Notitie*. Facsimile edition, 1984. Malta, Midsea Books Ltd.

Amadasi Guzzo, M. G. 2002. Iscrizione Punica a Cagliari. In P. Bernardini and A. Usai (eds.), *Quaderni della Soprintendenza archeologica per le provincie di Cagliari e Oristano*, 19: 173-9. Cagliari, Ministero per i Beni e le Attivita Culturali.

Ascough, R. S., Harland, P. A. and Kloppenborg, J. S. 2012. *Associations in the Greco-Roman World. A Sourcebook*. Texas, Baylor University Press and De Gruyter.

Azzopardi, G. 2017. *Ras il-Wardija sanctuary revisited. A re-assessment of the evidence and newly-informed interpretations of a Punic-Roman sanctuary in Gozo (Malta)*. Oxford, Archaeopress.

Bonanno, A. (with Cilia, D.) 2005. *Malta. Phoenician, Punic and Roman*. Malta, Midsea Books Ltd.

Bremmer, J. N. 2014. *Initiation into the Mysteries of the Ancient World*. Berlin / Boston, De Gruyter.

Brody, A. J. 1998. *"Each Man cried out to his God". The Specialized Religion of Canaanite and Phoenician Seafarers*. Harvard Semitic Monographs, 58. Atlanta (Georgia), Scholars Press.

Budin, S. L. 2014. Before Kypris was Aphrodite. In D. T. Sugimoto (ed.), *Transformation of a Goddess. Ishtar – Astarte – Aphrodite*. Orbis Biblicus et Orientalis, 263: 195-215. Fribourg and Göttingen, Academic Press Fribourg and Vandenhoeck and Ruprecht.

Busuttil, J. 2015. The Chrestion Inscription. *Treasures of Malta* XXI/2 (Easter 2015): 60-3.

Calabi Limentani, I. 1968. *Epigrafia Latina*. Milano-Varese, Istituto Editoriale Cisalpino.

Caruana, A. A. 1882. *Report on the Phoenician and Roman Antiquities in the Group of the Islands of Malta*. Malta, Government Printing Office.

Ciantar, G. A. 1772. *Malta Illustrata* I-II. Malta.
Cooley, A. E. 2012. *The Cambridge Manual of Latin Epigraphy*. New York, Cambridge University Press.
Crooks, S. 2013. *What are these Queer Stones? Baetyls: Epistemology of a Minoan Fetish*. British Archaeological Reports International Series, 2511. Oxford, Archaeopress.
Das, S. 2009. *Sacred Stones in Indian Civilization*. New Delhi, Kaveri Books.
De Vincenzo, S. 2013. *Tra Cartagine e Roma. I centri urbani dell' eparchia punica di Sicilia tra VI e I sec. a.C.* Berlin / Boston, De Gruyter.
Evans, A. J. 1901. Mycenean Tree and Pillar Cult and Its Mediterranean Relations. *The Journal of Hellenic Studies* 21: 99-204.
Evans, J. D. 1971. *The Prehistoric Antiquities of the Maltese Islands: A Survey*. London, The Athlone Press, University of London.
Falsone, G. 1993. An ovoid betyl from the tophet at Motya and the Phoenician tradition of round cultic stones. *Journal of Mediterranean Studies* 3/2 (1993): 245-85.
Franklin, J. C. (n.d.). Kinyras and the Musical Stratigraphy of Early Cypus. In G. Van Den Berg and T. Krispijn (eds.), *Musical Traditions in the Middle East: Reminiscences of a Distant Past*. (In press).
Gaifman, M. 2012. *Aniconism in Greek Antiquity*. Oxford Studies in Ancient Culture and Representation. Oxford, Oxford University Press.
Gatt, J. E. 1937. *A Guide to Gozo*. Malta.
Glinister, F. 2000. Sacred Rubbish. In E. Bispham and C. Smith (eds.), *Religion in Archaic and Republican Rome and Italy. Evidence and Experience*: 54-70. Chicago and London, Fitzroy Dearborn Publishers.
Gouder, T. C. 1978. Some Amulets from Phoenician Malta. *Heritage* 16 (November 1978): 311-5.
Jung, C. G. and Kerényi, C. 1969. *Essays on a Science of Mythology. The Myth of the Divine Child and the Mysteries of Eleusis* (trans. by R. F. C. Hull). Princeton (New Jersey), Princeton University Press.
Kerényi, C. 1976. *Dionysos. Archetypal Image of Indestructible Life* (trans. by Ralph Manheim). New Jersey, Princeton University Press.
Lincoln, J. S. 2003. *The Dream in Native American and Other Primitive Cultures*. Mineola (New York), Dover Publications, Inc.
Malone, C. 2009. Small Finds Catalogue. In C. Malone, S. Stoddart, A. Bonanno and D. Trump (with T. Gouder and A. Pace) (eds.), *Mortuary customs in prehistoric Malta. Excavations at the Brochtorff Circle at Xagħra*

(1987-94): 421-73. Cambridge, McDonald Institute for Archaeological Research, University of Cambridge.

Malone, C., Bonanno, A., Trump, D., Dixon, J., Leighton, R., Pedley, M., Stoddart, S. and Schembri, P.J. 2009. Material Culture. In C. Malone, S. Stoddart, A. Bonanno and D. Trump (with T. Gouder and A. Pace) (eds.), *Mortuary customs in prehistoric Malta. Excavations at the Brochtorff Circle at Xagħra (1987-94)*: 219-313. Cambridge, McDonald Institute for Archaeological Research, University of Cambridge.

Malone, C., Mason, S. and Stoddart, S. (with Kermorvant, A., Martínez-Cruz, B., Prat-Hurtado, F., Redhouse, D., Stove, C. and Trump, D.). 2009. Methods Applied in the Analysis of the Circle. In C. Malone, S. Stoddart, A. Bonanno and D. Trump (with T. Gouder and A. Pace) (eds.), *Mortuary customs in prehistoric Malta. Excavations at the Brochtorff Circle at Xagħra (1987-94)*: 63-78. Cambridge, McDonald Institute for Archaeological Research, University of Cambridge.

Malone, C., Stoddart, S., Trump, D. and Duhig, C. 2009. Żebbuġ Phase Levels: Spatial and Stratigraphic Analysis. In C. Malone, S. Stoddart, A. Bonanno and D. Trump (with T. Gouder and A. Pace) (eds.), *Mortuary customs in prehistoric Malta. Excavations at the Brochtorff Circle at Xagħra (1987-94)*: 95-107. Cambridge, McDonald Institute for Archaeological Research, University of Cambridge.

Mercieca, S. 2014. The Proserpina Temple and the History of its Chrestion Inscription. *Treasures of Malta* XXI/1 (Christmas 2014): 33-9.

Meyer, M. W. (ed.) 1999. *The Ancient Mysteries. A Sourcebook.* Philadelphia (Pennsylvania), University of Pennsylvania Press.

Minoja, M., Cossu, C. and Migaleddu, M. 2012. *Parole di Segni. L'Alba della Scrittura in Sardegna.* Sardegna Archeologica. Guide e Itinerari, 47. Sassari, Carlo Delfino editore.

Moore, J. P. 2000. *Cultural Identity in Roman Africa: The 'La Ghorfa' Stelae.* Unpublished PhD thesis, McMaster University.

Moscati, S. 1973. *The World of the Phoenicians* (trans. by Alastair Hamilton). London, Sphere Books Ltd.

Moscati, S. 2005. *Fenici e Cartaginesi in Sardegna.* Bibliotheca sarda, 102. Nuoro, Ilisso Edizioni.

Murray, M. A. 1923. *Excavations in Malta* I. London, Bernard Quaritch.

Murray, M. A. 1925. *Excavations in Malta* II. London, B. Quaritch.

Nielsen, I. 2014. *Housing the Chosen. The Architectural Context of Mystery Groups and Religious Associations in the Ancient World*. Contextualizing the Sacred, 2. Turnhout (Belgium), Brepols Publishers.

Nilsson, M. P. 1985. *The Dionysiac Mysteries of the Hellenistic and Roman Age*. Salem (New Hampshire), Ayer Company Publishers, Inc.

Pesce, G. 2000. *Sardegna Punica*. Bibliotheca sarda, 56. Nuoro, Ilisso Edizioni.

Prent, M. 2003. Glories of the Past in the Past: Ritual Activities at Palatial Ruins in Early Iron Age Crete. In R. M. Van Dyke and S. E. Alcock (eds.), *Archaeologies of Memory*: 81-103. Malden (MA), Blackwell Publishers Ltd.

Recchia, G. 2007. Il tempio e l'area sacra megalitica di Tas-Silġ: Le nuove scoperte dagli scavi nei livelli del III e II millennio A.C. In C. Panella (ed.), *Scienze dell'Antichita'. Storia, Archeologia, Antropologia* [12 (2004-2005)]: 233-62. Rome, Universita' degli studi di Roma «La Sapienza».

Spaeth, B. S. 1996. *The Roman Goddess Ceres*. Austin, University of Texas Press.

Stoddart, S., Malone, C., Mason, S., Trump, B. and Trump, D. 2009. The Tarxien Phase Levels: Spatial and Stratigraphic Analysis and Reconstruction. In C. Malone, S. Stoddart, A. Bonanno and D. Trump (with T. Gouder and A. Pace) (eds.), *Mortuary customs in prehistoric Malta. Excavations at the Brochtorff Circle at Xagħra (1987-94)*: 109-205. Cambridge, McDonald Institute for Archaeological Research, University of Cambridge.

Vella Gregory, I. 2005. *The Human Form in Neolithic Malta*. Malta, Midsea Books Ltd.

Wenning, R. 2001. The Betyls of Petra. *BASOR* 324: 79-95.

Yeates, S. J. 2008. *The Tribe of Witches. The Religion of the Dobunni and Hwicce*. Oxford, Oxbow Books.

# General Index

**A**
'Abdmĭlkot, 57, 72
Abdosir, 71
Abode, 1, 3, 47
Acanthus, viii, 55, 62
  - Foliage, viii, 55, 62
Acropolis, 40, 65
Aegean, 1, 32
  - Area, 32
  - Traditions, 1
Afterlife, 41-2
Agents, 4
  - Of concealment, 4
*Agora*, 36
Agricultural, 45
Agrigento, v, 11
Alkamenes, 40
Altar/s, vi-vii, 10, 15, 22-3, 25, 31, 35-7, 47, 69
  - Tripillar (altar/s), vi-vii, 36-7, 69
Amazons, 47
Amphora, v, 11
  - Red-figure (amphora), v, 11
Amulet/s, vii, 41-2, 75
  - (Pillar-) amulet, vii, 41
Analogy/ies, 4, 6, 8, 65
  - Ethnographic (analogy/ies), 4, 6-8
Ancestor/s, 3, 15, 18, 20
  - Dead (ancestor/s), 3, 15, 18, 20
Aniconic, vi, viii-ix, 1, 3, 4, 9, 18, 32-4, 43, 47, 50, 54, 60, 65, 67

  - Betyl/s, 43, 60, 65
  - Character, 67
  - Cult/s, vi, viii, 32-4, 54, 67
  - Form/s, 4
  - Object/s, 65
  - Representation/s, 1, 3, 4, 18, 47, 50
  - Stone/s, 9
Aniconism, vii, 3, 4, 9, 34, 52-3, 69, 75
  - Empty space (aniconism), 3
  - Material (aniconism), 4
Animated, 1, 9
  - Pillar, 9
  - Stones, 1
Animation, 9
Anna Chiara Fariselli, 47
Anthropomorphic, 3, 9, 32
  - Imagery, 9
  - Representations, 3
Anthropomorphised, v, 1-2, 69
Anthropomorphism, 52
Apex, 26, 55
  - Tapering (apex), 55
Aphrodite, 12, 47
Apollo, 10, 47
  - Carinus, 47
Apollon, viii, 61-2
  - Agyieus, viii, 61-2
Apologist, 4
  - Christian (apologist), 4
Apulian, v, 11
Arcadia, 39

Archaic, 67, 75
 - Representation, 67
Architectural, 43, 71, 77
 - Element, 43, 71
Ares, 47
Ark, 65
 - Of the Covenant, 65
Arkadia, 39
 - Hellenistic (Arkadia), 39
Artemis, 64
Artistic, 4
 - Representation, 4
Astarte, 43
Athena, 64
Athenian, 40
Attica, 39
 - West (Attica), 39
*Augusti libertus*, 64, 72
Augustus, 66
Aventine, 39
 - Hill, 39

**B**

Baal, 57, 59-60
 - Hammon, 59-60
Ba'al Chammàn, 36, 39
Baalshamim, 59-60
Ball, 15
Balonag, 57
Barracks, viii, 64
 - Military (barracks), viii, 64
Basin, 23, 30-2, 50, 55
Bench/es, 49-50
Bethel, 9
Betyl/s, v-ix, 1, 2, 4, 5, 7-8, 10-13, 15, 17, 19, 26, 29-32, 35, 41-3, 45-52, 54-5, 59-63, 65-9, 71-2, 75, 77
 - Amulet/s, 41
 - Aniconic (betyl/s), 43, 60, 65
 - (Betyl-)like, 26
 - Bottle-shaped (betyl/s), 4
 - Column (betyl/s), vii, 51-2, 54
 - Cone-shaped (betyl/s), 12, 67
 - Cylindrical (betyl/s), 30
 - Gilded (betyl/s), 63
 - Miniature (betyl/s), 41
 - Paired (betyl/s), 8, 59
 - Prehistoric (betyl/s), 55, 69
 - Pyramidal (betyl/s), vii, 45-9, 52, 54
 - Relief (betyl/s), 69
 - Representation/s, viii, 12, 61-2
 - Stone (betyl/s), v, 2, 10, 17, 19, 50
 - Vase-shaped (betyl/s), v, 5
Biblical, 9, 10, 73
Bilingual, viii, 55-6, 71
 - Inscription/s, viii, 55-6, 71
Binġemma, 7, 41
Birth, 61
Birżebbuġa, vi, 29, 35
Black Sea, 47
Bod'aštart, 57, 72
Bone/s, 26, 41
 - Animal (bone/s), 26
Borġ in-Nadur, vi, 7, 8, 26, 29-30, 33, 35-6
 - People, 36
 - Temple, vi, 26, 29-30, 35
Britain, 39, 40
British, viii, 57, 64
 - Museum, 57
Bronze, v, 12, 65-7
Bronze Age, 8, 10, 29, 33
 - Pottery, 29

Bud/s, 55, 60-1
- Flower/ing (bud/s), 55, 60
- Lotus (bud/s), 55, 61
Bust, 42
Byblos/ian, viii, 9, 12, 67-9
- Phoenician (Byblos), 69
- Phoenician city of (Byblos), 68

C

Cabras, vi-vii, 26, 30, 38, 47-8
- Archaeology Museum of (Cabras), vi-vii, 26, 30, 38, 47-8
Cagliari, v, viii, 2, 55, 58-60, 72, 74
Calabria, 66
Candelabra, 57
Canopic (jars), 4
Capo delle Colonne, 66
Capo San Marco, vii, 45, 47-8
Caracalla, 67
Carla del Vais, 47
Caroline Malone, v, 17
Carthaginian/s, ix, 45
- Goddess/es, 45
Cavity/ies, vii, 49-50, 52
- Conical (cavity/ies), vii, 49-50, 52
Celestial, 68
- Deity, 68
Ceres, 39
Chain, 48
- Fragment, 48
- Metal (chain), 48
Chammanim, 36, 40
Charles de Brochtorff, 22
Chert, 36
- Flake of (chert), 36
Chrestion, viii, 63-4, 66, 72, 74, 76

Christian, 4, 12, 68
- Early (Christian), 12, 68
- Writer/s, 12, 68
Cippus/i, vii-viii, 45-6, 55-60, 72
- Maltese (cippi), 57, 59
- Marble (cippus/i), viii, 55-8
- Punic (cippus), 55
- Pyramidal (cippus), vii, 46
Citadel/s, vii, 41, 64
Classical, 10, 15
- Period, 10
Claudian, viii, 61-2
- Period, viii, 61-2
Clement of Alexandria, 4
Coastal, 45
- Cliff, 45
- Promontory, 45
Coelius, 66
Coin/s/age, v, viii, 10, 12, 48, 67, 69
Collars, 43
Column/s/ar, vii, 10, 17, 27, 32, 49-52, 54, 60-1, 66, 72
- Betyl/s, vii, 51-2, 54
- (Column-) shaped, 17
- Drums, 60
- Form, 61
- Stone (column), 50
- Wooden (column), 66
*Columna aurea*, 66
Complex, 15, 17, 21-3, 26, 29, 54-5
- Burial (complex), 15, 17, 21
- Main (complex), 23, 26
- Sanctuary (complex), 29, 54-5
- Temple (complex), 22-3, 26
Component/s, 64-5
- Temple (components), 64-5

Cone/s/ical, vi-vii, 8, 12, 15, 22-4, 26, 32, 34, 43, 49-50, 52, 61, 67
- Cavities, vii, 49-50, 52
- (Cone-)shaped, 12, 43, 61, 67
- Stone/s, vi, 22, 24, 26
- Stone (cone/s), 22-3, 34

Consecration, 9

Context/s, viii-ix, 1, 4, 6-8, 10, 15, 18, 20, 32, 41-3, 47, 49, 55, 57, 60-2, 65, 77
- Early historic (contexts), 7

Corradino, 7, 55, 71
- Hill, 7, 55

Cosa, 40

Crete, 36, 76
- Southern (Crete), 36

Criteria, 7, 43

Criticism, 12, 68

Crown, 43

Cruciform, vii, 50, 52-4
- Figure/s, vii, 50, 52-3
- Herm/s, vii, 52, 54

Cult/s/ic, v-vi, viii, 1, 3, 6-7, 10, 12, 15, 20, 23, 26, 29, 32-4, 39, 54, 64-5, 67, 75
- Ancestor (cult/s), 15
- Aniconic (cult/s), vi, viii, 32-4, 54, 67
- Context/s, 6
- Figurine/s, 32
- Figurine-based (cult/s), vi, 32-4
- Function/s, 6
- Image/s, 3
- Of Proserpina, 67
- Place/s, 1
- Practice/s, 10
- Significance, 1, 7
- Statue/s, v, 1, 12, 65
- Stone/s, 6, 26, 75
- Stone (cult/s), 6, 15
- Structure/s, 23
- Worship, 32, 34

Culture/s, ix, 6, 59, 75-6

Cushion, 10

Cylindrical, 22, 30
- Betyls, 30
- Stones, 22

Cyprus, 10, 67

## D

Dabar, 57

Daniel Cilia, vi, viii, 20, 56

Decoration, 22-3, 59
- Drilled (decoration), 23
- Pitted (decoration), 22

Dedicated, viii, 7, 12, 43, 59, 60, 63-4, 66-8, 71-2
- Statues, 7, 59-60

Dedication, viii, 43, 55-60, 66
- Inscribed (dedication), 59
- Object of (dedication), 43, 59-60

Dedicator/s, 57

Dedicatory, 57, 59-60
- Inscription/s, 57, 59-60

Delphi, 9

Demeter, 36, 39
- Malophoros, 36
- Eleusinian (Demeter), 39

Demonic, 1
- Power, 1

Deposit/s/ion/s, 20, 26, 48, 50, 54, 61
 - Structured (deposit/s/ion), 26, 48, 50, 54
Desacralisation, 20, 61
 - Exercise, 20, 61
Diffusionism, 6
Dionysios, 71
Dionysus, 39, 65
 - Cadmus, 65
Divine, ix, 1, 4, 10, 36, 39, 65-6, 75
 - Manifestation, 10
 - Presence, ix, 4, 65-6
Divining block, 22, 25
Divinity/ies, 10, 18, 39
 - Minor (divinities), 39
Djed, vii, 41-2
 - Pillar/s, vii, 41-2
Dual/ity, 59, 61
 - Form/s, 59, 61
Dwejra, 7, 45

## E

Eastern, 22, 26, 29, 32, 69
 - Extraction, 69
 - Origins, 69
 - Phenomenon, 69
Egyptian, 4, 60
 - Ancient (Egyptian), 4
Eiromos, 66
El, 9
Element/s, vi, ix, 4, 6-8, 33, 43, 71
Eleusinian, 39
Eleusis, 39, 75
El-Gabal, v, 12, 67
Emesa, v, 12, 67, 69, 74
 - Syrian (Emesa), 69

Enclosure, viii, 12, 67-8
 - Sacred (enclosure), viii, 12, 67-8
Ephesus, 65
Epigraphy, 59, 75
Epitome, 59
Eusebius, 9, 66, 73
Evans (see: John Evans)
Evolution, vii, 52-3
Excavation/s, 36, 47, 75-7
Excavators, 30, 45, 50
Extra-urban, 8

## F

Fertility, 39, 60-1
 - Aspect, 60-1
Figural, 4, 13
 - Forms, 4
 - Representations, 4
 - Statues, 13
Figurative, 3, 4, 20, 69
 - Images, 3, 4, 69
 - Imagery, 4
 - Representation/s, 3, 69
 - Version, 20
Figurine/s, vi, 4, 32-4, 54
 - (Figurine-)based, vi, 32-4
 - Fragments, 32, 54
Finial, 61
 - Cone-shaped (finial), 61
Firmicus Maternus, 12, 68, 73
Flavian, 66
 - Dynasty, 66
Flint, 36
Foliage, viii, 55, 59-62
 - Decoration, 59

Formulaic, 57, 59
- Similarity, 59
Fosse Temple, 36
Fragmentation, 30
France, viii, 55-6
Freedman, 66, 72
- Of Augustus, 72
- Of the emperor, 66
Freestanding, 8
Frieze, 57
Function/s, ix, 1, 6-7
Funerary, viii, 1, 4, 10, 15, 20-1, 42, 45, 47, 60-2
- Context/s, viii, 4, 15, 20, 42, 47, 60-2
- Cult practices, 10
- Inscription, 45
- Sphere, 1

## G

Gades, 61
Gate of the Nymphs, 47
Genealogy, 57
*Genii cucullati*, 39
Geographer, 8, 47
Geographical, ix, 4, 6
- Boundaries, ix, 4
- 'Compartments', 4
- Regions, 4, 6
Germany, 39
Ġgantija, vi-vii, 7-8, 16, 20, 22-4, 32-4, 41-2, 69
- Phase, 8, 22, 32-4, 69
- Temples, vi, 22, 24, 41
- Temples Visitors' Centre, vi, 20, 23

Gilded, 63-5, 72
- Ark of the Covenant, 65
- Image, 64
- Statue/s, 64
God/s, v, vii, 1, 9-10, 12, 18, 36, 41, 54, 66-7, 74
- Of the Mountain (see: El-Gabal)
Gozo, v-vii, 7, 15, 17-20, 22-4, 41, 45, 49, 51, 53, 64, 72-5
- Archaeology Museum, vii, 41, 45
Graces, 39
Grand Harbour, 55
Greece, 8, 9-10, 39, 47, 64-6, 68, 73
- Ancient (Greece), 39, 47, 64-5
Greek/s, viii, 4, 8-10, 12, 39, 47, 55-6, 68, 71, 73, 75
- Antiquity, 12, 75
- Version/s, 55, 71
Gymnasium, 47

## H

Ħaġar Qim, vi, 7, 23, 27-8, 33
- Temples, vi, 7, 23, 27-8
Ħal Saflieni, vi, 7, 18, 21, 33
- Hypogeum, vi, 7, 18, 21, 33
Hannibal, 66
Hanno, 57, 72
Headland, 45
- Sanctuary, 45
Heavenly, 66
*Hederae distinguentes*, 66
Hekate, 40
- Epipyrgidia, 40
Hellenistic, 39, 77
Hera, viii, 12, 67-8

Heracles, viii, 55-6, 59-61
Herakles, 71
Herm/s, v, vii, 3, 15, 52, 54
  - Cruciform (herm/s), vii, 52, 54
  - Semi-figural (herm/s), 3, 15
Hermes, vii, 54
Hirom (see: Eiromos)
Historic, vi, ix, 6-7, 31-2, 34, 69
  - Early (historic), ix, 6-7, 69
  - Period/s, vi, 7, 31-2, 34, 69
  - Times, ix, 6
Humanised, 52
*Hwicce*, 39-40, 77
  - Tribe, 39-40
Hypogeum (see: Ħal Saflieni Hypogeum)

# I

Iconic, 34, 39
  - Form, 39
Iconism, vii, 52-3
Iconographic, 6-9
  - Element/s, 6-8
  - Evidence, 7, 9
Identical, viii, 17-18, 20, 55-6
Identity/ies, 20, 76
Igneous, 59
Image/s, 3-4, 39-40, 43, 60, 64-5, 69, 75
  - (Image-)based, 34
Imitation, 52
Imperial, viii, 8, 43, 59, 66-7
  - Family members, 43, 59
Incense, 57
Incubation, 18

Industrial, 65
  - Contexts, 65
Inscription/s, viii, 1, 6-7, 10, 39, 41, 43, 45, 55-7, 59-61, 63-6, 71-2, 74, 76
  - Bilingual (inscription), viii, 55-6, 71
  - Commemorative (inscription), 63, 66
  - Neo-Punic (inscriptions), 57
  - Punic (inscription/s), viii, 43, 45, 55-7, 71-2
Inspiration, 26
Interchangeable, 18, 57
  - Positions, 57
Interpretative, 4
  - Framework, 4
*Isola di San Pietro*, 59, 61
Israel/ite/s, 36, 65-6
  - Ancient (Israelites), 65
  - King, 66
Italian, 40
Italy, viii, 39, 61-2, 65-6, 75
  - South/ern (Italy), 39, 66
Ivy leaf, 66
  - Motifs, 66

# J

Jacob, 9
Jane L. Ainsworth, 60
Jason Gibbons, v, 17
John Evans, 35
Jordan, 8
Joseph Shaw, 36
Judaism, 9
Juno, 66
Jupiter, 66

## K
Kommos, 36
Kordin, 7, 26, 33
Kore, 39

## L
Lacinium, 66
Lacish, 36
*Lacunae*, 8
Levantine, 1
Libation, 22
   - Holes, 22
Liber, 39
Libera, 39
Lilybaeum, 39
Literary, 6-7, 9-10
   - Parallelism, 10
   - Reference, 9
Literature, 64
Litholatry, 1
Location/s, 1, 6-8, 45
Log, 65
   - Of Dionysus Cadmus, 65
Lotus, 41, 55, 60-1
   - Buds, 55, 61
   - Flower, 41, 60
Louis XVI, 55
Louvre Museum (in Paris), viii, 55-6

## M
Macrinus, 68
Magical, 1
Magna Graecia, 39
Maktar, 57
Maltese, v-vi, viii-ix, 6-8, 15, 17, 32-4, 55, 57, 59-61, 63, 65, 69, 75
   - Aniconism, 69
   - Chronology, v, 8
   - Cippi, 57, 59
   - Islands, v, viii-ix, 6-7, 15, 32, 34, 55, 63, 69, 75
M.A. Murray, 35
Marble, viii, 55-8, 71-2
Marker/s, 4, 18
Market-place, 64
Marsala, 39
Marsaxlokk, vi, 7, 29, 31, 55
Materiality, 4
*Matres*, 39
Meaning/s, ix, 6, 60
Mediterranean, 7, 32, 47, 75
   - Context, 47
   - Eastern (Mediterranean), 32
Megalithic, 16, 32
   - Temple, 32
Megara, 47, 65
*Melite*, viii, 64
Melqart, viii, 55-61, 71-2
   - Of Tyre, viii, 57-8, 71-2
Memorial, 1, 47
   - Marks, 1, 47
Menander, 66
Mercury, 39-40
Meteorites, 1
Methodology, 4
Michelangelo Cagiano de Azevedo, 55
Miniature, vii, 41-2
   - Betyls, 41
   - Form, 42
   - Pillar/s, vii, 41-2
*Missione Archeologica Italiana*, 45, 73
Mithraic, 68
Mithras, 12

Mnajdra, vi, 7, 26, 28, 33
- Temples, vi, 7, 26, 28
Monument/s, 39, 47
- Non-figural (monuments), 47
Monumentality, 65
Mortar, 29, 65
Mortuary, 1, 75-7
- Contexts, 1
Motya, v, 5, 75
Mtarfa, viii, 7, 63-5, 72
- Hill, viii, 63-5
Murray (see: M.A. Murray)
*Museo Archeologico Nazionale* of Cagliari, v, viii, 2, 55, 58
Museo Archeologico of Agrigento, Sicily, v, 11
*Museo Civico* of Padova, viii, 61-2
Museo del Vicino Oriente, Sapienza University, Rome, v, 5
Museo Nazionale Romano Palazzo Massimo, Rome, v, vii, 3, 54
Mushroom, 61
- (Mushroom-)shaped, 61
Mutilation/s, 20, 61
- Deliberate (mutilation/s), 20, 61
Mythical, 60
- Rebirth, 60

**N**

Nabataean/s, 1, 9
National Museum of Archaeology (in Valletta), viii, 55-6
Near East, 13
Necropolis, vii, 39, 42, 45, 47-8, 60
Neolithic, 8, 15, 69, 77
- Period, 8, 15, 69

Neo-Punic, 57
- Inscriptions, 57
*Nephesh*, 1
Niche/s, v-vii, 5, 15-16, 22-4, 26, 35-6, 38, 50, 53
Non-figural, ix, 4, 47
Nora, 4, 39, 45, 50, 60
- Necropolis of (Nora), 60
Numismatic, 13
- Imagery, 13
Nymphs, 39, 47

**O**

Obelisk/s, 22-3, 65
- (Obelisk-)like, 22-3
Ochre, v, 15, 17
- Red (ochre), v, 15, 17
Offering/s, vii-viii, 9, 45, 47-50, 52, 55-7, 59, 71
- Table, vii, 45, 47-50, 52
Oil, 9
- Olive (oil), 9
Old Testament, 9-10, 73
Open-air, 9
- Sanctuaries, 9
Orient/al, 42, 47
- (Oriental-)style, 42
Ornamentation, 6
Orthostat, 26
Osiris, 41
Osirxamar, 71
Ostia, 65
Ouaz, 41
- Pillar, 41
Ouranos, 9
Ovoid, 8, 55, 57, 75
- Profile, 55, 57

## P

Padova, viii, 61-2
Pagan, 4, 12, 68, 73
   - Imagery, 4
   - Perspective, 4
Paintings, 10
Pair/s, 8, 17, 50, 55, 59
Palmette, 57
   - Motifs, 57
Panhellenic, 9
   - Shrine, 9
Paphos, 12, 67
Parallelepiped, 59
   - Block, 59
Paris, viii, 55-6
Parish, 22
   - Church, 22
Pausanias, 8-10, 39, 47, 65, 68, 73
Pedestal/s, v, vii, 11, 45-6, 55, 57, 59
Pediment/s, 43, 72
Persephone, 39
Petra, 8, 77
Pharae, 10, 68
Phenomenon/a, ix, 4, 6, 9-10, 69
   - Eastern (phenomenon), 69
Philo (of Byblos), 9
Phoenician/s, ix, 8, 36, 41, 66, 68-9, 74-6
   - Period, 41, 69
   - Tradition/s, 36, 69, 75
Pigment, 23
   - Red (pigment), 23
*Pila*, 64-7
Pillar/s, v-vii, 8-10, 15-17, 19, 21-4, 26, 29, 32-4, 36, 41-3, 45, 60, 65-6, 69, 71-2, 75
   - Anthropomorphised (pillars), 69
   - Cone-shaped (pillar), 43
   - Djed (pillar/s), vii, 41-2
   - Free-standing (pillars), 10
   - Golden (pillar/s), 66
   - Imagery, 10
   - Miniature (pillar/s), 41
   - Niche, 26
   - Ouaz (pillar), 41
   - (Pillar-)amulet, vii, 41
   - (Pillar-)like, v, 8, 15, 17, 26
   - Square (pillar), 45
   - Stone (pillar/s), v-vi, 16-17, 19, 21-4, 26, 34
Pillow, 9-10
Plaque, 39
   - Stone (plaque), 39
Plaster, 45
Plebs, 39
Plinth, 47
Pliny the Elder, 9, 73
Plug, 57
   - (Plug-)like, 57
Poles, 36
Polytheistic, 9-10
Portable, 8
Position/s, 6-8, 57
Practice/s, ix, 6, 10
Precinct, 20, 48, 50
   - Sacred (Precinct), 20, 48, 50
Prehistoric, vi, ix, 6-8, 15, 17, 21-2, 31-4, 41, 55, 69, 75-7
   - Betyl/s, 55, 69
   - Contexts, 7-8, 15
   - Temple/s, vi, 22, 31-3, 41
Priests/ly, 17
   - Role, 17
Priestess/es, 17-18

Primeval, 47
  - Past, 47
Primitive, 3, 15, 75
  - Version, 15
*Procurator*, viii, 63-4, 72
Promontory, 45
  - Coastal (promontory), 45
Proserpina, viii, 63-5, 67-8, 72, 76
Protection, 41-2, 61
Provenance, 55
'ps-yaton, 71
Psychological, 6
  - Mechanisms, 6
Pula, 4
Punic, vi-viii, 8, 26, 30, 36, 38, 41, 43, 45, 50, 55-8, 69, 71-2, 74
  - Cippus, 55
  - Inscription/s, viii, 43, 45, 55-8, 71-2
  - Late (Punic), 45
  - Period, 8, 41
  - Tophet/s, vi-vii, 26, 30, 36, 38, 50
  - Traditions, 69
Pyramid/idal, vii, 39, 45-9, 52, 54
  - Betyl/s, vii, 45, 47-9, 52, 54
  - Cippus, vii, 46
  - Shape, vii, 45-6
  - Stone/s, vii, 45, 47-8

## Q
Qrendi, vi, 27-8

## R
Rabat (Malta), 7, 41
Ras il-Wardija, vii, 7, 45-9, 51-4, 74
Rebirth, 41, 60-1
  - Mythical (rebirth), 60
Receptacle, 57
Red-figure, v, 10-11
Relief/s, v-vii, 4-5, 26, 30, 36, 38-9, 43, 55, 60, 69
  - Betyl, v-vi, 4-5, 26, 30, 43, 69
  - Tripillars, vii, 36, 38
Religion/s, 9-10, 12, 68, 73-5, 77
  - Polytheistic (religion), 10
Religious, 1, 6-7, 15, 26, 29, 43, 60, 69, 77
  - Context/s, 6-7, 15, 43, 60
  - Experience, 1
  - Ideology, 29
  - Significance, 1
  - Site, 69
  - Tradition, 26
Renovation/s, viii, 63-4, 66
  - Works, viii, 63-4
Repairs, viii, 63-4, 66
Representation/s, viii-ix, 1, 3-4, 6, 12, 18, 36, 39, 47, 50, 61-2, 67, 69, 75
  - Minted (representations), 12
Ribbon, v, 11
Ring/s, 10, 60
Ritual/s, ix, 1, 6, 10, 18, 20, 22, 30, 32, 48, 50, 61, 77
  - Activity/ies, 32, 77
  - Behaviour, 1
  - Cleansing, 30
  - Context/s, ix, 1, 10, 18, 20, 61
  - Dreaming (rituals), 18
  - Functions, 6
  - Use, 48, 50, 61
Roman/s, viii-ix, 1, 8, 10, 12-13, 39-40, 45, 61-2, 66-7, 69, 72, 74, 76-7
  - Betyl, viii, 62

- Coinage, 12, 67
- East, 1
- Emperors, 66
- Historian, 12, 67
- Imperial period / times, viii, 8, 66-7
- Inscription, 72
- Late (Roman), 40, 45
- Malta, 69
- Period, 8, 40
- Provinces, 13
- Rule, 12
- Times, 10, 45, 67, 69

Rome, v, vii, 3, 5, 39, 54, 66, 75
Rudimentary, 1, 3
Rural, 8, 64-5
- Character, 65
- Temple, 64

## S

Sabatino Moscati, 45, 52
*Sacello Triolo Nord*, vii, 36-7
Sacrality, 15
Sacred, viii, 1, 6, 9, 12, 15, 20, 22, 36, 48, 50, 67-8, 75, 77
- Character, 20, 22, 48
- Enclosure, viii, 12, 67-8
- Objects, 50
- Precinct, 20, 48, 50
- Stone/s, 1, 6, 9, 15, 75
Sa Mandara, v, 2
Samassi, v, 2
Santa Gilla, viii, 55, 58, 72
Sant' Antioco, vii, 42, 50, 59
Šapot, 57, 72
Sarapion, 71

Sardinia/n, v-viii, 2, 4, 7, 26, 30, 36, 38, 42, 45, 47-8, 50, 55, 58-61, 72
Scenario, 6, 32
- Island (scenario), 6
Schematic, 50, 52
- Cruciform figures, 50, 52
- Symbol, 50
Seals, 10
Seasons, 39
Seat, 3-4
- Vacant (seat), 3-4
Selinunte, vi-vii, 36-7
Semi-anthropomorphic, vii, 50, 52-3
- Figure/s, vii, 50, 52-3
Semi-anthropomorphised, v, 15, 17, 26
Semi-figural, ix, 3-4, 15, 52
- Form, 52
Semi-iconic, 4
Semitic, 9
Shape/s, vii, 8, 15, 22, 42, 45-6, 49, 65
- Natural (shape), 8
Shrine/s, vi, viii, 9, 12, 16, 35-6, 47, 67-8
- Imageless (shrines), 47
- Tripillar (shrine/s), vi, 35-6
Sicily, v-vii, 7, 11, 36-7, 39
Sicyon, 47, 64
Significance, 1, 7, 10, 23, 45
Skirt/s, 17-18
- Design, 17-18
Skorba, 8, 32, 69
- Red (Skorba) phase, 8, 32, 69
Sleeping lady, 18

Social, 6
Solar, 36
  - God, 36
Solomon, 66
Solunto, 36
Sotakos, 9
Space, 3-4, 36, 45, 50
  - Empty (space), 3-4
Spain, 61
  - Southern (Spain), 61
Sphere/s/ical, v, 1, 8, 15, 18, 21-3, 26, 32, 34, 65, 72
  - Stone/s, v, 8, 15, 18, 22, 26
  - Stone (sphere/s), 15, 21, 23, 26, 34
Spiral, vii, 49, 51
Stability, 41
Star, 68
  - Symbol, 68
Statue/s, v, 1, 4, 7, 10, 12-13, 15, 17, 22-3, 43, 59-61, 64-6
  - Cult/ic (statue/s), v, 1, 12, 65
  - Dedicated (statues), 7, 59-60, 66
  - Figural (statues), 13
  - Schematised ('statues'), 1
Statuette/s, 15, 17-18, 20, 26, 61
Stela/ae/ai, v-vii, 4-5, 10, 26, 30, 36, 38-9, 50, 57, 59, 76
  - Standing (stelai), 10
  - Triple (stela), 39
Steven Ashley, v, 17
Structured, 26, 48, 50, 54
  - Deposit/ion, 26, 48, 50, 54
Stylistic, 59
  - Similarity, 59
Substitute, 9, 65

Sulcis, 42, 50, 59
Sun-dial/s, 65
Sun god, v, 12, 67
Survival, viii, 41, 67, 69
Symbol/s, 1, 41, 50, 60-1, 68
Syria/n, v, 12, 67, 69

**T**

Tacitus, 12, 67, 73
Tanit, 45, 50
Tarxien, vi, 7-8, 15, 21-2, 25, 32-4, 77
  - Phase, 8, 15, 21, 32-4, 77
  - Temple/s, vi, 7, 22, 25
Tas-Silġ, vi, 7, 29-31, 33, 36, 41, 43, 48, 55, 60, 69, 71, 77
  - Sanctuary, vi, 29, 31, 36, 48, 55
*Ta' Trapna ż-Żgħira*, v, 7, 15, 17, 32
Tell Qasile, 36
*Temenos*, 45
  - Wall, 45
Temple/s, v-viii, 1, 7-8, 12-13, 21-33, 35-7, 39, 41-2, 45, 47-9, 52, 54, 63-8, 72, 76
  - Component/s, 64-5
  - Juno's (temple), 66
  - Maltese (temple/s), vi, 33, 65
  - Period, 8, 32
  - Renovated (temple), 66
  - Rural (temple), 64
  - Site/s, 21, 45
  - (Temple) 300, 36
Temporal, ix, 4
Terminal/s, 61
Termination, 20, 48, 50, 54
Terrace/s, vii, 45, 47, 49-51, 54

Textual, 57
- Parts, 57
Tharros, vi-vii, 26, 30, 38-9, 42, 45, 47-8
- Necropolis, vii, 39, 42, 45, 47-8
Theban, 65
- Acropolis, 65
Thelpusa, 39
Thespians, 8
Tithe, 9
- Offerings, 9
Titus Flavius Clemens (see: Clement of Alexandria)
Tomb 5, 15
Tomb XXVI, 60
Tophet/s, v-vii, 4-5, 26, 30, 36, 38-9, 42, 50, 59, 75
Torpedo, vi, 26, 30
- (Torpedo-)like, vi, 26, 30
Trachyte, 59
Tradition/s, 1, 26, 34, 36, 69, 75
Trajanic, 66
- Period, 66
Transitional, vii, 52-3
- Stage, vii, 52-3
Traveler, 8, 47
Treatment, 6-7, 15, 43, 45, 49, 59-60, 65
- Special (treatment), 15, 43, 60
Triad/s/ic, 36, 39
- Cult, 39
- Divine (triad/s), 36, 39
Triangle, 50
Tripillar/s, vi-vii, 35-40, 69
- Altar/s, vi-vii, 35-7, 69
- Arrangements, 40
- Shrine/s, vi, 35-6
Triple, 36, 39-40
- Form, 39-40
- Groups, 39
- Image/s, 40
Triplicate, 39
Triplicity, 40
Tryggve Mettinger, 4
Tunisia, 57
Turkey, 65
Twin/s, vi, 16, 20, 55, 59, 61, 71
Twin-seated, vi, 16, 20
- Figures, vi, 16, 20
Tyre/ian, viii, 57-8, 66, 71-2
- Phoenician (Tyre), 66

**U**

Uranius Antoninus, 67
Urban, viii, 8, 64
- Centre, viii, 64

**V**

Valletta, viii, 7, 55-6
Varrese Painter, v, 11
Vase/s, v-vi, 4-5, 10, 18, 20
- (Vase-)shaped, v, 5
Veneration, 4, 13, 47
- Objects of (veneration), 13
- Of stones, 4
Vertical, 55, 57
Victoria, vii, 7, 41
Visual, 59
- Culture, 59
Volcanic, 59
- Rock, 59

Votive, 30-1, 39

**W**
Wool, 9
Worship, vii, ix, 1, 12, 32, 34, 45, 47, 49, 68
 - Stone (worship), ix, 1, 12, 45, 47, 68

**X**
Xagħra, v-vii, 7, 15-20, 22-4, 32, 41, 75-7
 - Brochtorff Circle, v-vi, 7, 15-20, 22, 32, 75-7
Xewkija, 7, 22, 33
Xlendi, 7, 45

**Z**
Żebbuġ, v, 8, 15-17, 32-4, 69, 76
 - Phase, 8, 15-16, 32-4, 69, 76
Zeus, vi, 9, 36-7, 47
 - Meilichios, vi, 36-7
 - Meilichius, 47